THE SOLID EARTH

Theme: Constancy and Change

GET READY TO

OBSERVE & QUESTION

How do rocks bend?

Rocks are used by people to make buildings and monuments. In nature, rocks may also build hills and mountains. How do forces both inside Earth and on its surface create structures such as the one shown?

EXPERIMENT & HYPOTHESIZE

How can fossils help tell us how old a rock is?

Make your own series of rock layers—with fossils in the layers. The order of the layers along with the fossils they contain are clues to the ages of the rocks.

INVESTIGATE!

RESEARCH & ANALYZE

As you investigate, learn more from these books.

- **Rocks, Minerals, and Fossils** by Keith Lye (Silver Burdett Press, 1991.) Ever wonder how you can tell the difference between jewelry made of glass and that made of real diamonds? This book will tell you how to find out.

Our World
ROCKS, MINERALS AND FOSSILS
Keith Lye

- **My Side of the Mountain** by Jean Craighead George (Puffin Books, 1991). What would it be like to live in the mountains? Read this book for one person's story.

WORK TOGETHER & SHARE IDEAS

How can you build an organized mineral collection?

Working together, you'll begin a collection of rocks, fossils, and minerals. Then you will share your new knowledge with others by creating a museum-type display of your collection and by publishing a guide to local rocks, fossils, and minerals.

MINERALS

Have you ever visited a jewelry store or a museum and admired jewelry containing gemstones such as rubies or diamonds? Have you ever seen bracelets or necklaces made of shiny metals such as silver or gold? Both gemstones and metals have something in common. They are *minerals*.

Prospecting for Gold

The Alaska gold rush of 1898 brought a flood of hopeful prospectors to the North. Alaska still boasts of some hardy individuals who search for gold in rugged, remote areas. Three such people are Paul and Grace Byrd and their daughter, Blyss. During the summer, the family prospects for gold in Bonanza Creek, a stream in southeastern Alaska's Wrangell-St. Elias National Park. The Byrds use a portable suction machine to suck up stones and sand from the creek bottom. The reward for their hard work is finding about 28 g (1 oz) of gold per day.

Gold is just one of a group of substances called minerals. Minerals vary greatly in appearance and texture. Sparkling diamonds, gleaming gold, and graphite are all minerals. What properties make something a mineral? Through the investigations in this chapter, you'll find out.

Coming Up

◀ The Byrd family prospecting for gold in Alaska

HOW CAN YOU IDENTIFY MINERALS?

A mineral is a solid element or compound from Earth's crust that has a definite chemical composition and crystal shape. Now see if you can name this mineral. It is most often black or brown. It's used in tools for drilling. It's highly prized when it is colorless or blue-white. If you said diamond, you are right!

Activity

The Way Minerals Look

Think about it—you identify most things just by looking at them. Minerals aren't any different. When you get to know them, you'll be able to look at them and name them. The key is getting to know them.

MATERIALS

- cardboard egg carton
- mineral set
- marker
- white unglazed ceramic tile
- *Science Notebook*

Procedure

1. Use your egg carton to store your mineral specimens. Open the carton and use the marker to number the pockets from 1 through 12.

2. **Observe** each mineral specimen. Does each look like it is made up of all the same kind of material? Is there any evidence of crystal structure in the minerals? **Record** your observations in your *Science Notebook*.

Step 1

3. Make a chart like the one shown, with 8 columns and 12 rows. Any columns you don't fill in during this activity will be filled in during later activities.

MINERAL PROPERTIES CHART							
Mineral Number	Luster	Color	Streak	Hardness	Cleavage	Special	Name

4. The way a mineral reflects light is called **luster** (lus'tər). Some minerals reflect light well—they appear shiny. They have a *metallic* luster. Those that don't have a metallic luster have a *nonmetallic* luster. Separate your mineral specimens into two sets, one set that looks shiny like metal (such as brass, gold, or iron) and the other that doesn't look like metal.

Step 5

5. Put each mineral in your egg carton. As you do it, write on your chart *metallic* or *nonmetallic* under *Luster* and opposite the number of the pocket.

6. Inspect each mineral specimen and write its color in the next column of your chart. If needed, use more than one word, such as *yellow-brown* or *brass yellow*.

7. When a mineral is ground to a powder, its color is called its **streak**. **Predict** each mineral's streak. With each mineral, try to make a mark (like a pencil mark) on the tile. The color of the mark is the color of the streak. **Record** each mineral's streak in your chart.

Analyze and Conclude

1. Compare the color and streak of each mineral in your collection. What conclusions can you draw about the color and streak of a mineral?

2. How are the properties of streak and luster useful in getting to know minerals?

INVESTIGATE FURTHER!

RESEARCH

You use two minerals every day in your classroom. In fact, you use them for their streak. Find out what they are.

Activity
Scratching Minerals

You may have noticed that some minerals are harder than others. Hardness is an important property in identifying minerals. Geologists test a mineral's hardness by seeing what objects will scratch or be scratched by the mineral. Try this scratch test yourself.

MATERIALS
- goggles
- mineral set in egg carton from previous activity
- Mineral Properties Chart
- pane of glass, 8-cm square
- steel nail
- copper wire, 10 cm in length
- *Science Notebook*

SAFETY
Put on goggles. When using the glass, keep it flat on the desk. Press the mineral specimen onto the glass and pull it across the glass. DO NOT HOLD THE GLASS IN YOUR HAND.

Procedure

1. Try scratching one mineral with another; do just a little scratch. Don't scrub the minerals together or you'll damage them. Can you find the hardest mineral in your set? How about the softest? **Record** your findings in your *Science Notebook*. Remember to return each mineral to its numbered pocket.

2. Geologists often use a set of tools to judge the hardness of a mineral. The tools include a piece of glass, a fingernail, a steel nail, and a piece of copper. **Predict** which of these items will be the hardest. Then scratch each tool with the others to rank the tools from softest to hardest.

3. Try to scratch each mineral with the edge of your fingernail. Always rub your finger over a mark to make certain it's a scratch and not a streak. A streak will rub off, but a scratch won't. If your fingernail scratches the mineral, write $H < F$ ("hardness is less than a fingernail") for that mineral in your chart.

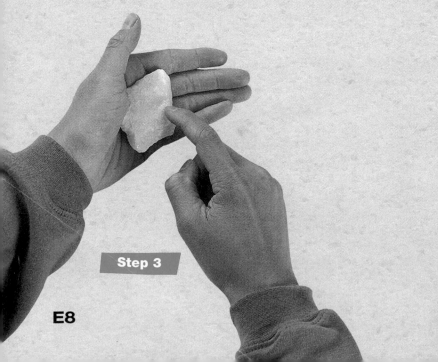

Step 3

Step 4

E8

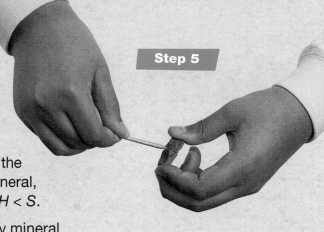

4. Find out if the copper wire will scratch the minerals that your fingernail did not scratch. For those that the copper scratches, write $F < H < C$ ("hardness is greater than a fingernail but less than copper").

5. Now try the steel nail on those minerals that the copper didn't scratch. If the nail scratches the mineral, write this in the chart, using an S for "steel": $C < H < S$.

6. Finally, try scratching the glass plate with any mineral that was not scratched by the steel. **Record** those that scratch the glass as $H > G$ ("hardness is greater than glass").

Analyze and Conclude

1. What was the order of hardness for your hardness tools?

2. Did your predictions match your results? Which mineral did you find to be the hardest? Which was the softest? **Compare** your results with those of your classmates. Did your classmates get the same results? If not, repeat the test and compare.

Step 6

INVESTIGATE FURTHER!

RESEARCH

One of the important properties of gemstones is that they are hard. After all, you wouldn't want to wear a gem if it scratched easily. Look up the hardness of diamonds, rubies, sapphires, emeralds, topaz, and garnets. How do they compare? What scale is used to compare hardness?

Activity

Minerals That Break Funny

MATERIALS
- salt
- hand lens
- mineral set
- Mineral Properties Chart
- *Science Notebook*

If you have ever broken some glass, you were probably more concerned with cleaning it up than with how the glass broke. However, the way something breaks can tell us something important. Find out how minerals break.

- - - - - - - - - - - - - - - - - - -

Procedure

1. Observe some salt with a hand lens. Can you see the flat sides? They are called **cleavage** (klēv′ij) planes. The salt crystals always break along their cleavage planes. Pick out a large crystal and try to crush it with your pencil. How are the pieces like the original crystal? **Record** your observations in your *Science Notebook*.

Step 1

2. Observe some large salt crystals with a hand lens. Can you see cleavage planes inside the crystals? They often look like cracks. The cracks look as though the crystal might break along them. Sometimes you can see cleavage planes inside a crystal when you can't find them on the outside.

3. Observe your mineral samples. Can you find any that have flat surfaces where the mineral has broken? The surfaces are probably cleavage planes. Can you see cleavage planes inside the mineral? If you find one or more cleavage planes on a mineral, write *yes* under *Cleavage* in your chart.

Analyze and Conclude

1. List the minerals that have cleavage planes.

2. **Compare** your mineral observations with those of your classmates. Do you agree on which minerals show cleavage? **Hypothesize** why you did or did not get the same results.

Activity
Name That Mineral

MATERIALS
- mineral set
- Mineral Properties Chart
- *Science Notebook*

Now that you can recognize mineral properties, you can find out the name for each of the minerals in your mineral set.

Procedure

1. Take mineral number 1 from its pocket in the egg carton. Use your chart to review the properties of the mineral.

2. Refer to the "Properties of Minerals" table on page E19. Look at the left column. Notice that it divides the table into two sections, minerals with metallic luster and minerals with non-metallic luster. In which section of the table does your mineral belong? **Record** your observations in your *Science Notebook*.

3. Now move to the second column in the table. It is for hardness. How hard is your mineral? Find the section of the table that describes the hardness of your mineral. Remember to stay in the section for the luster of your mineral when finding the hardness.

4. Move from left to right through the columns of the table. Information about streak and cleavage is sometimes in the column labeled *Special*. You should find the name of the mineral in the right-hand column. Write its name in the last column of your chart.

5. Repeat steps 1–4 for all the other minerals in your set.

PROPERTIES OF MINERALS

Luster	Hardness	Color	Streak	Special	Name
Metallic	Harder than glass	Black	Black	magnetic	MAGNETITE
Metallic	Harder than glass	Brassy yellow	Black	"fools gold"	PYRITE
Metallic	Softer than glass	Steel gray	Red or reddish brown	may have reddish patches	HEMATITE
Metallic	Softer than steel	Brassy to gold yellow	Black	often has blue, red & purple tarnish	CHALCO-PYRITE
Metallic	Harder than a fingernail	Silver gray	Gray to black	heavy, shows cleavage	GALENA

Luster	Hardness		Color	Special	Name
Non-metallic	Harder than glass		white, pink, gray	hardness is very close	FELDSPAR
Non-metallic	Harder than glass	yes			AMPHIBOLE
Non-metallic	Harder than glass	yes (2)			PYROXENE
Non-metallic	Harder than glass	no			
Non-metallic	Softer than steel	yes (6)			
Non-metallic	Softer than steel	yes (4)	purple, yellow		
Non-metallic	Softer than copper	yes (3)	white, pink	crystal faces are usually curved	
Non-metallic	Softer than copper	yes (3)	colorless, white, yellow	cleavage planes make parallelograms	CAL...
Non-metallic	Softer than a fingernail	yes (3)	colorless, white	tastes salty, breaks in cubes	HALITE
Non-metallic	Softer than a fingernail	yes (1)	colorless, white	sometimes transparent	GYPSUM
Non-metallic	Softer than a fingernail	yes (1)	colorless, silvery, black	peels in thin sheets, can be green	MICA
Non-metallic	Softer than a fingernail	yes (1)	light green to white	usually flakey	TALC
Non-metallic	Softer than a fingernail	no	yellow to brown	looks like rust	LIMONITE
Non-metallic	Softer than a fingernail	no	red	earthy	HEMATITE

Analyze and Conclude

1. Were you able to find the name of each of your minerals? **Hypothesize** why you were or were not able to find all of the minerals' names.

2. How are properties useful in identifying minerals?

Mineral Properties

Did you know that the "brain" of a computer, called a computer chip, is made from a mineral found in beach sand? A **mineral** is a solid element or compound from Earth's crust that has a definite chemical composition and crystal shape. Minerals can look very different from one another—colorless like quartz, silver or red like hematite, or shiny like gold and silver—but we find ways to use them all.

Look around and you'll see minerals being used. People may be wearing jewelry made of a gemstone like a ruby, an emerald, or an opal. The walls in your home are probably made of wallboard, which is gypsum sandwiched between layers of paper. The windows in your classroom are made from quartz. The body powder you use may be made from the mineral talc. When you talk to a friend on the telephone, copper wires transmit your voice. Your lunch may be wrapped in aluminum foil, made from the mineral bauxite. Perhaps you can think of other minerals you use every day. How many are there?

Why are minerals used in so many ways? They have different properties that make them right for many different uses. These same properties help scientists tell minerals apart, just as they helped you in the activities. What are some of the properties of minerals you examined in the activities?

▲ The mineral gypsum is used to make wallboard, or drywall.

▲ Talc is a mineral that you may sprinkle on your skin after a shower.

▲ A mineral's luster is a clue to its identity. Silver, at left, has a metallic luster. Fluorite, right, has a nonmetallic luster.

Luster

Luster is one property that can be used to classify minerals. **Luster** refers to the way light reflects from the surface of a mineral. Look at the graphite in your pencil or at a piece of silver or gold jewelry. The shiny appearance of these minerals is called metallic luster. Any mineral that reflects light like polished metal has a metallic luster. All other minerals have nonmetallic luster. Minerals that have nonmetallic luster vary in the way they look. For example, the luster of a nonmetallic mineral may be dull like cinnabar, pearly like mica, or glassy and brilliant like diamond.

Hardness

A mineral's **hardness** is a measure of how easily it can be scratched. Talc is the softest mineral. It can be scratched by all other minerals. Diamond is the hardest mineral. It can scratch the surface of any other mineral, but no other mineral can scratch a diamond.

You can estimate a mineral's hardness by using Mohs' scale, shown in the table below. This scale lists the hardness of

MOHS' SCALE OF MINERAL HARDNESS		
Mineral	**Hardness**	**Simple Test**
Talc	1	easily scratched by fingernail
Gypsum	2	scratched by fingernail
Calcite	3	barely scratched by copper
Fluorite	4	easily scratched by steel knife
Apatite	5	scratched by steel knife
Orthoclase feldspar	6	scratches glass with difficulty
Quartz	7	scratches glass and steel
Topaz	8	scratches quartz
Corundum	9	no simple test
Diamond	10	no simple test

ten common minerals. To test a mineral for hardness, find out which mineral on the scale is the hardest one that your mineral scratches. For example, a mineral that can scratch calcite but can't scratch fluorite has a hardness between 3 and 4. Also, just as you did in the activity on page E8, you can use your fingernail, copper, steel, glass, and the simple scratching tests listed in Mohs' scale to estimate hardness. What would be the hardness of a mineral that can be scratched by copper but not a fingernail?

Hardness is caused by the arrangement of matter in a mineral. For example, both diamond and graphite consist only of carbon. One arrangement produces the hardest natural mineral (diamond), and the other arrangement produces one of the softest minerals (graphite).

Color

Another mineral property is color. The elements making up a mineral determine its color. For example, chromium gives ruby its unusual red color. Although color is the easiest mineral property to observe, it's not the most reliable for identifying minerals. Many different minerals have similar colors. Some minerals vary in color due to the presence of tiny quantities of other substances. Pure quartz is colorless, but traces of other substances can make it become white, pink, or purple.

Streak

Most minerals aren't as hard as a ceramic tile. When you scratch a mineral against a tile called a streak plate,

SCIENCE IN LITERATURE

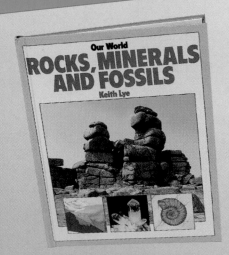

ROCKS, MINERALS AND FOSSILS
by Keith Lye
Silver Burdett Press, 1991

Read about fool's gold and true gold on page 25 of *Rocks, Minerals and Fossils* by Keith Lye. Make a table to summarize all the tests that can be done to tell these two minerals apart. Make sure you include the expected results of each test.

When you're done, browse through this colorful reference book. You'll find it's easy to locate information that interests you by looking at the pictures, reading the large titles, or using the index. For example, if you're not sure what makes a mineral different from a rock, look on page 13. There's a photo of a rock, called granite, and the four kinds of minerals that make it up.

some minerals crumble off as a powder. The color of this powder is the mineral property called **streak**.

The streak of most minerals is either colorless or the same color as the mineral. However, for a few minerals, the color of the mineral and the color of the streak aren't the same. For example, if you scratch silver-colored hematite on a streak plate, you find its streak is red! Apatite is a dark mineral with a white streak. Pyrite is brassy yellow and leaves a greenish-black streak. Which of the minerals that you tested had a colored streak?

▲ **A mineral's streak may be different from its color.**

Cleavage

Some minerals split easily along flat surfaces, a property called **cleavage**. If you have ever handled mica, you know how easily it splits apart. Mica breaks along cleavage surfaces that are all in the same direction. Some minerals have cleavage surfaces in more than one direction. The salt you observed in the activity on page E10 is the mineral halite. Its cube shape occurs because halite splits along cleavage surfaces in three directions.

You may think that gemstones break naturally along several cleavage surfaces. But most gemstones do not break along cleavage surfaces. Therefore, gem cut-

▲ **Calcite can be cleaved in three directions, or planes.**

▲ **Rubies, like many other gemstones, have no cleavage.**

▲ **Mica cleaves along one plane, and peels in thin sections.**

ters must grind the gems to create the flat, shiny faces, called facets, that give gems their different shapes.

Using Mineral Properties

How are mineral properties useful? If you were a gold miner, using the properties you just learned about might make you a fortune! You would need mineral properties to tell gold from other minerals you find.

Compare the samples of gold and pyrite shown. At first glance they may seem alike. Notice that they both have a brassy yellow color. They both also have a metallic luster, and neither mineral has cleavage.

Pyrite is known as fool's gold. Based on color, luster, and cleavage alone, you might easily mistake pyrite for gold. A smart gold miner would also compare the minerals' hardness and streak. Pyrite has a hardness of about 6 and gold has a hardness of about 3. Pyrite leaves a greenish-black streak; gold's streak is golden-yellow. Gold has a greater value than pyrite, so it pays to be able to tell them apart. ■

▲ Pyrite, shown here, has some properties similar to those of gold.

▲ Gold, shown here, is softer than pyrite and has a different streak.

UNIT PROJECT LINK

Start a collection of minerals. There are many ways to get mineral samples. You could join a mineral club. There may be some adults in your community who are collectors and would be happy to help you. You could write to students in schools in other parts of the country and trade minerals through the mail. Or you could go out and collect local mineral samples from road cuts and streambeds. To determine the name of any unknown minerals in your collection, see the activity on page E11.

Identifying Minerals

A key is an organizer designed to help you identify things. The table on page E19, "Properties of Minerals," is a key designed to help you identify minerals. To identify an unknown mineral, match the properties you observe in your sample with the properties listed in the table.

Let's try an example. Say you are given the unknown mineral shown below. What is it?

Using the Table: Nonmetallic Minerals
Step 1. Luster
Is it metallic or nonmetallic?

What kind of luster does your mineral have? It doesn't look like polished metal, so it's nonmetallic. Find in the table the column labeled *Luster*, and locate all the nonmetallic minerals.

Step 2. Hardness
What scratches it?

If you had your mineral sample in front of you, you would use the materials from the activity on page E8 to test for hardness. The sample can be scratched with a fingernail. Locate this under the column labeled *Hardness*. Notice that there are only six minerals in the table that are both nonmetallic and softer than a fingernail. Your sample must be one of those six.

Step 3. Cleavage
Is there any? In how many directions?

You can see that your sample does have cleavage in one direction. You can

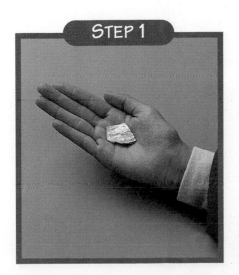

STEP 1

STEP 2

STEP 3

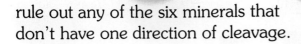

rule out any of the six minerals that don't have one direction of cleavage.

Step 4. Color
What is it?

Observe that your sample is colorless. Look under the column labeled *Color* and notice that two minerals fit the bill: mica and gypsum. Which is it?

Step 5. Special Properties
Are there any?

Find the *Special* column. Since your sample peels easily in thin sheets, as is listed for mica, it must be mica. How might the procedure vary for a metallic mineral? Let's try it for the sample shown.

Using the Table: Metallic Minerals

Step 1. Luster
Is it metallic or nonmetallic?

Notice that the sample looks like polished metal. You can rule out all nonmetallic minerals, so cover the part of the table that shows nonmetallic minerals.

Step 2. Hardness
What scratches it?

If you could test it, you'd find that your sample can't be scratched by glass. Look in the table to see which metallic minerals are harder than glass. Notice that there are only two minerals with this property: magnetite and pyrite.

Step 3. Color
What is it?

Observe that your sample is black. Look under the column labeled *Color* and notice that pyrite is brassy yellow. Your mineral must be magnetite. But to make sure, check its other properties.

Step 4. Streak
What is it?

If you could scratch your sample along a streak plate, you would see that its streak is black. This agrees with the data in the table under the column labeled *Streak*.

Step 5. Special Properties:
Are there any?

If you had a magnet, you would see that your sample is attracted to it. You can use this property and others in the table to confirm that your unknown sample is indeed magnetite. ■

STEP 1

STEP 4

STEP 5

PROPERTIES OF MINERALS

Luster	Hardness	Color	Streak	Special	Name
Metallic	H > G	black	black	magnetic	MAGNETITE
Metallic	H > G	brassy yellow	black	fool's gold	PYRITE
Metallic	S < H < G	steel gray	red or reddish brown	may have reddish patches	HEMATITE
Metallic	C < H < G	brassy to gold yellow	black	often has blue, red, and purple tarnish	CHALCO-PYRITE
Metallic	F < H < G	silver gray	gray to black	heavy, shows cleavage (3)	GALENA

Luster	Hardness	Cleavage	Color	Special	Name
Non-metallic	H > G	yes (2)	white, pink, gray	hardness is very close to glass	FELDSPAR
Non-metallic	H > G	yes (2)	black, green	cleavage planes make a diamond shape	AMPHIBOLE
Non-metallic	H > G	yes (2)	black, green	cleavage planes make a square shape	PYROXENE
Non-metallic	H > G	no	colorless, white, pink, smoky, purple	looks glassy, chips or breaks like glass	QUARTZ
Non-metallic	C < H < S	yes (6)	yellow to brown or black	yellowish white streak	SPHALERITE
Non-metallic	C < H < S	yes (4)	purple, green, yellow	crystals are cubes, transparent	FLUORITE
Non-metallic	F < H < S	yes (3)	white, pink	crystal faces are usually curved	DOLOMITE
Non-metallic	F < H < S	yes (3)	colorless, white, yellow	cleavage planes make parallelograms	CALCITE
Non-metallic	H < F	yes (3)	colorless, white	tastes salty, breaks in cubes	HALITE
Non-metallic	H < F	yes (1)	colorless, white	sometimes transparent	GYPSUM
Non-metallic	H < F	yes (1)	colorless, silvery, black	peels in thin sheets, can be green	MICA
Non-metallic	H < F	yes (1)	light green to white	usually flaky	TALC
Non-metallic	H < F	no	yellow to brown	looks like rust	LIMONITE
Non-metallic	H < F	no	red	earthy	HEMATITE

*Numbers in parentheses give number of cleavage planes.

Key: H—hardness; G—glass; S—steel; C—copper; F—fingernail; <—less than; >—greater than.

Diamonds

Have you ever passed a jewelry store window filled with sparkling diamond rings? Just what are diamonds and how do we get them? Diamond is the hardest mineral. It is made of pure carbon. It forms deep underground, where temperature and pressure are very great, in a rock called kimberlite (kim′bər līt). Most kimberlite forms long, tube-shaped rock bodies called pipes. Sometimes these pipes reach Earth's surface.

Mining Diamonds

Diamonds have been discovered in many different parts of the world. The map shows areas that have provided the greatest number of diamonds. A limited number have been found in the United States, in northern California, southern Oregon, Arkansas, and the eastern Appalachian Mountains.

Most diamonds are found in stream deposits called placers. A placer is a deposit of sediment that contains important mineral fragments. Diamond placers form when streams flow over kimberlite pipes and carry kimberlite particles downstream. Because diamonds are heavier than other rock particles, they drop to the bottom of streams and build up on stream beds. Miners remove diamonds in the same way gold is panned.

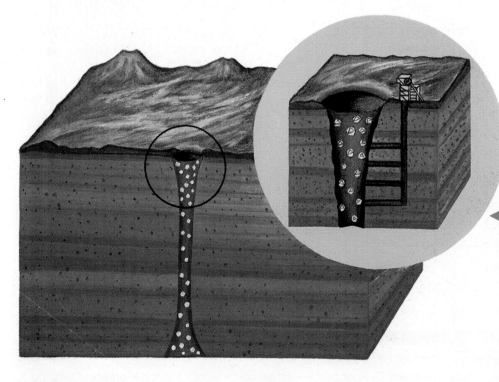

◄ In South Africa, mine shafts are dug into kimberlite pipes and diamonds are removed. Such mines are the world's richest sources of diamonds.

Diamonds are also mined directly from kimberlite. This is done by digging either surface pits or deep underground mine shafts. Once removed from the ground, the kimberlite is crushed and the rock is washed away, leaving behind only the harder diamonds. Any remaining traces of kimberlite are separated and removed by machines.

After mining, diamonds are sorted according to quality. Only two out of every ten diamonds are of good enough quality to be made into jewels. The rest are cut up for other uses, like making abrasives, glass cutters, rock drill bits, and telecommunication products. The better-quality diamonds are then sorted, or graded, according to their color, size, and purity.

A Cut Above

After grading, diamonds are sent to a gem cutter. Gem-quality diamonds are cut because doing so shows off their brilliant nonmetallic luster. Next, the diamond is shaped. Finally, it is polished by holding it at an angle to a spinning disk coated with diamond dust. This step creates the sparkling facets, or faces, highly prized in gemstones. ■

▲ **Raw diamonds are often found in kimberlite.**

▲ **Gem cutters cut and polish selected diamonds.**

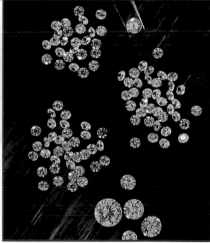

▲ **Finished diamonds are sold around the world.**

INVESTIGATION 1

1. Describe how you would use mineral properties to distinguish quartz from calcite.

2. When trying to identify an unknown mineral, list all the questions you would need to ask and answer about that mineral.

WHAT ARE MINERALS USED FOR?

Look around at your classmates. How many are wearing jewelry? You know that minerals are used to make much of that jewelry. Try to name as many minerals (think in terms of gems and metals) used in jewelry as you can. Can you think of other uses for minerals?

Activity

Growing Crystals

Mineral crystals are used in jewelry and in electronics. Some of these crystals are grown in laboratories. In this activity you can grow your own crystals!

Procedure

1. Fill a 500-mL jar with hot water from the tap. Dissolve as much alum as possible in the water (about 100 grams, or 3–4 oz). Cap the jar and let it stand overnight.

2. Pour a small amount of the solution from the jar into the bottom of a bowl and let it stand overnight. The next morning you should find some small crystals in the bowl. Use the spoon to remove one or two good crystals and pour the solution back into the jar.

3. Tie one of the crystals to the end of a piece of thread. Suspend the crystal in the baby-food jar.

4. Nearly fill the baby-food jar with solution from the large jar. Be careful not to pour any crystals into the baby-food jar. Tent a piece of paper over the jar to keep dust out. **Predict** about how much the crystal will grow each day.

MATERIALS

- goggles
- gloves
- glass jar, 500 mL, with cap
- hot tap water
- alum
- shallow bowl
- plastic spoon
- polyester thread
- large baby-food jar
- sheet of paper
- scissors
- metric ruler
- *Science Notebook*

SAFETY /////

Wear goggles and gloves at all times. Be sure to wash your hands after handling the alum.

5. **Observe** your crystal growing. It may take a few days. Each day, **estimate** the size of the crystal. If the level of solution in the jar goes down, add more. When the crystal stops growing, remove it from the solution and **draw** a picture of it in your *Science Notebook*.

Step 3

Analyze and Conclude

1. About how large was the crystal when you started?

2. How large was the crystal when you stopped growing it?

3. How many days did the crystal grow?

4. Did your crystal grow by the same amount each day? Describe your evidence.

5. Think of ways people use crystals. **Infer** why scientists might want to grow crystals in a laboratory.

INVESTIGATE FURTHER!

EXPERIMENT

You can grow crystals from other substances. Instead of alum, try sugar, Epsom salts, or rock salt. Compare the shape of the crystals and how easy they were to grow.

Quartz
A Versatile Mineral

If you've ever been to a beach or seen pictures of one, you know that beaches are made of sand. The words *sand* and *gravel* really refer to the size of a grain of mineral or rock, sand particles being smaller than gravel. Any rock or mineral can be broken into sand-sized or gravel-sized pieces.

The most common sand in the world is quartz sand. Quartz is also one of the most important minerals. It is made of only two elements, silicon and oxygen. The colors and names of common types of quartz include clear (rock crystal), pink (rose), white (milky), and gray (smoky). Some forms of quartz are semiprecious gemstones such as amethyst, tigereye, and citrine.

Native Americans used one form, flint, for tools such as arrowheads.

Building With Quartz

Quartz plays an important role in the building industry. Many building materials are made of rocks and minerals. **Concrete**, for example, is a rock material made of sand and gravel and a binder. The binder, called portland cement, is made by grinding limestone and shale, two kinds of rock, into a powder. This powder is baked at high temperature until it forms balls called clinker. Cooled clinker is crushed to a powder and mixed with gypsum, another mineral. This mixture is then mixed with quartz-rich sand, gravel, and water and allowed to harden to form concrete. How have you seen concrete used in your neighborhood?

From left to right: clear quartz, rose quartz, milky quartz, smoky quartz ▶

▲ Concrete, a building material, is made with quartz and other minerals.

▲ Without quartz, there would not be glass.

Seeing With Quartz

Quartz is also used to make glass. By ancient times, people in the Middle East had a good understanding of quartz and its properties. Glassmaking probably began about 4,000 years ago in Egypt or Mesopotamia. Today the art of glass-making is a worldwide industry.

Glass is easy to make if you have the proper tools. Powdered quartz is mixed with powdered limestone and soda (not the kind you drink, but a solid substance called sodium carbonate). The mixture is heated to about 1,600°C (2,912°F). At this temperature it melts. Then it is cooled quickly so that crystals cannot form. Crystals would make objects seen through the glass look wavy and deformed. Very old glass looks wavy because it has begun to crystallize. Look around you. How many ways can you see glass being used?

The Computer Mineral

Quartz can be separated into its two parts, silicon and oxygen. From the silicon, crystals can be grown (much as you did in the activity on pages E22 and 23) and later cut into thin pieces. These pieces of pure silicon are used in

◀ Quartz, a compound of silicon and oxygen, is one of the most abundant minerals in Earth's crust.

E25

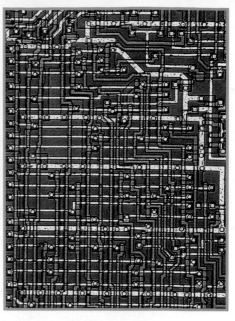

The brain, of every desktop computer (*left*) is a silicon chip. Many chips, each the size of a fingernail, are obtained from silicon wafers (*center*). Each chip is etched with the electronic circuits (*right*) that carry out the calculations that make computers such time-savers.

the electronics industry, which is a major part of the world's economy. Computer chips, which are the brains of our computers, and solar cells, which power solar calculators, are made with silicon.

Perhaps the most amazing thing about quartz crystals is that they generate electricity. If the crystals are squeezed, they bend slightly and produce electricity. In addition, when a small electrical current is put through a crystal, it vibrates. The vibrations are very regular, making quartz crystals ideal for keeping time. Tiny quartz crystals are used to keep time in many types of watches.

Maybe you thought quartz was something you walked on as you viewed the ocean. But a world without window glass, portable electronic games, radios, CD players, computers, or concrete would be hard to imagine! ■

◄ You may be carrying a quartz crystal on your wrist. In watches with a quartz crystal, the crystal's vibrations keep time more accurately than those watches that use a spring to keep time.

How Iron Becomes Steel

In Arizona, there is a huge hole in the ground known as the Barringer Meteorite Crater. Scientists hypothesize the crater formed about 25,000 years ago when an 18-m (59-ft) wide chunk of iron from space collided with Earth. The chunk of iron from space shows that iron isn't found only on Earth. It's all over the universe! Maybe it should be called the universal metal!

Iron occurs in minerals. Magnetite and hematite are important iron-containing minerals. Minerals from which metals can be removed are called **ores**. An iron ore is made up of iron and other elements.

The most widespread source of iron is hematite, an ore made up of iron and oxygen. Over 2 billion years ago, hematite layers began to build up in the oceans. Over time the hematite was covered by layers of sediment. Later, parts of the ocean bottom were slowly lifted up to the surface, and the iron deposits eventually became exposed. That was the easy part! For us, the hard part is getting the iron ores out of the ground and the iron out of the ores.

Iron ore is mined all over the planet. In the United States, most of the iron we use comes from hematite mined in Canada and South America. Magnetite

Iron is used to make many different products such as the blades of skates (*left*), the rails of roller coasters (*center*), and the hulls of ships (*right*).

is not as easy to find as hematite, but it's a purer source of iron. The world's largest magnetite mine is in Sweden. Others are located in Wyoming, New York, Utah, South Africa, Austria, Italy, and Russia.

The process of removing metal from ore is called **smelting**. The first smelting of metal may have occurred about 9,000 years ago. Around 3,500 years ago, iron smelting became widespread. Iron was often used in making cooking tools and weapons. Because the intro-

duction of iron affected cultures so greatly, that period of time was called the Iron Age. The diagram shows how pig iron is made.

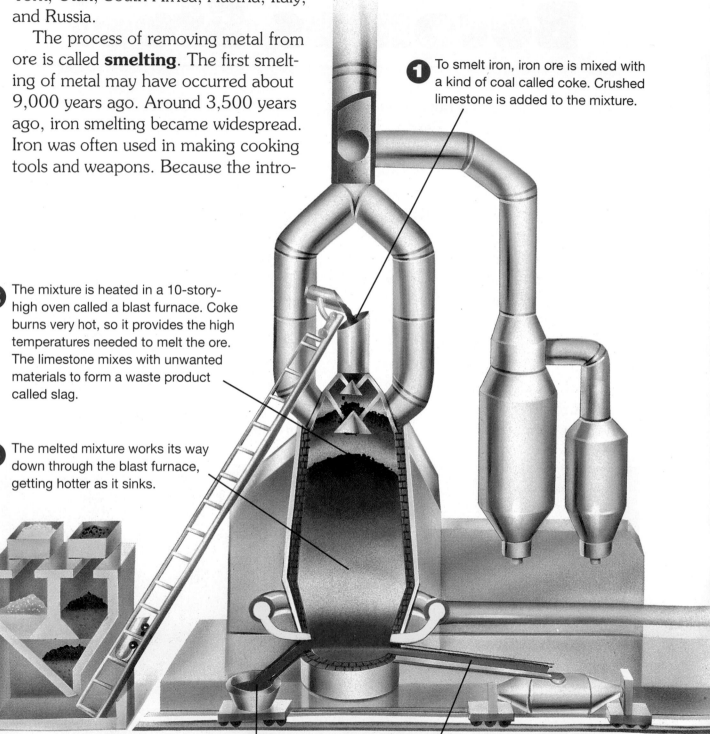

1 To smelt iron, iron ore is mixed with a kind of coal called coke. Crushed limestone is added to the mixture.

2 The mixture is heated in a 10-story-high oven called a blast furnace. Coke burns very hot, so it provides the high temperatures needed to melt the ore. The limestone mixes with unwanted materials to form a waste product called slag.

3 The melted mixture works its way down through the blast furnace, getting hotter as it sinks.

4 Wastes that are less dense separate and float on the molten metal. This slag is drained off.

5 The remaining melted iron, called pig iron, is drained from the bottom of the blast furnace.

▲ **Pig iron is remelted and mixed with a small amount of iron, making steel.**

Because of impurities such as carbon present in pig iron, it is too brittle to be used for purposes requiring great strength. Instead it is remelted and poured into molds. Iron made in this way is called cast iron. Cast iron is used to make bells, wood stoves, bathtubs, railings, and other products.

Pig iron can also be remelted and converted into steel. In a furnace, melted pig iron is brought to a high temperature. Air is blown over the iron to increase the heat and remove excess carbon. When the metal is free of carbon, a measured amount of carbon is mixed in. It may seem strange that carbon is removed only to be added again, but an exact amount of carbon is needed to make useful steel. Too much carbon makes the steel brittle and too little makes it weak.

▲ **Steel can be produced in a variety of forms, including rolled sheets.**

Steel can be rolled into sheets or made into bars, blocks, and other shapes. It can be made as sharp as a razor or as blunt as a hammer. Other metals can be added to steel to make alloys, or mixtures of metals. For example, chromium is added to make steel resist rusting. Nickel is added to make steel stronger. Titanium makes steel more resistant to heat. Tungsten makes steel strong at high temperatures.

How did you get to school today? If you came by public transportation, car, or bike, steel helped you. What other uses for steel can you think of? ■

▲ **The liquid steel is poured into molds and allowed to cool.**

E29

A World of Minerals

Mineral resources are in the ground all over the world. But they are not distributed evenly. As the map shows, some countries have more mineral resources than do others.

A country can mine its resources and use them to make products. The country can then sell some of its raw resources and products to other countries. The selling countries are called producers. Countries with few mineral resources must buy many resources or products. These buying countries are consumers. Consumers often buy raw resources to make products. If they sell these products to producers, the producers may actually be buying back their raw resources in a new form.

Worldwide Metal Resources

◇ TIN
○ BAUXITE
✖ LEAD & ZINC
◖ GOLD
△ SILVER
★ COPPER
■ IRON

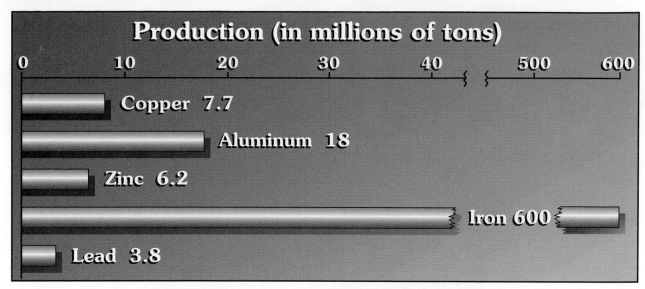

Production (in millions of tons)

0	10	20	30	40	500	600

Copper 7.7
Aluminum 18
Zinc 6.2
Iron 600
Lead 3.8

▲ **Worldwide yearly production of selected metals**

For example, raw iron ore may be shipped from the United States to Japan. A Japanese company turns the ore into iron, the iron into steel, and the steel into bike frames. Some frames are sold in Japan and some are sold in other parts of the world, including the United States.

Minerals and mineral products are an important part of the world trading market. There are few places on Earth where iron or steel isn't used in some way. Aluminum is important to canning and cooking industries. Silver is valued for jewelry. What other ways are mineral resources used in the world?

Why Waste?

The uses of mineral resources are unlimited. The amount of mineral resources is not. Although most mineral resources are fairly abundant, finding new sources is getting more difficult. And mineral resources are being used up fast. Your old tricycle may be buried in the middle of a landfill right now. Cars sit rusting in junkyards and on roadsides. Aluminum cans float on ocean waves where they were thrown. Usable mercury gets thrown away inside dead dry-cell batteries. These items are not really gone from our environment. They're still here but they're scattered, making it almost impossible for them to be recovered and reused.

Recycling Mineral Resources

Many communities in the United States have laws stating that certain

▲ **Much of Earth's mineral wealth ends up in places like this.**

▲ **The recycling of minerals helps keep their cost down.**

World Issues

World Issues

The way that mineral resources are handled in one country can affect many other countries. Look at the map on page E30 and the bar graph on page E31 and discuss answers to the following questions with your classmates.

Which two metals are produced in the largest quantity? Do you think the U.S. has to import such resources? What happens when a nation doesn't have enough raw resources or money to trade evenly? What happens when countries are in competition for a product in limited supply? What happens if a country holds back on selling raw resources or products needed by other countries of the world? ■

items must be recycled. In addition to nonmineral products like paper and plastic, metals such as copper, steel, brass, and aluminum are being recycled. Recycling doesn't totally solve the problem of using up a mineral resource, but it does extend our use of such resources.

Many people on the planet still don't recycle, so we slowly but surely lose valuable mineral resources. As a resource becomes scarce, its price rises. Eventually a new resource must be used in its place. Could the same cycle be repeated with the new resource?

INVESTIGATE FURTHER!

TAKE ACTION

Write to a local recycling center to find out which minerals can be recycled in your community. Then organize a recycling drive of those materials.

INVESTIGATION 2

1. Name six products made from minerals and at least one mineral used to make each product.

2. If you were building a house, list the materials made from minerals that you would use and explain why you would use them.

REFLECT & EVALUATE

WORD POWER

cleavage
concrete
hardness
luster
mineral
ores
smelting
streak

On Your Own
Review the terms in the list. Then use as many terms as you can to write a brief summary of the chapter.

With a Partner
Make up a quiz using all the terms in the list. Challenge your partner to complete the quiz.

BUILD YOUR PORTFOLIO

Make an illustrated chart that shows minerals and products made from those minerals.

Analyze Information

Observe the properties of the mineral sample shown. This mineral's streak is gray to black. The mineral cannot be scratched with a fingernail but can be scratched by glass. Use the "Properties of Minerals" table on page E19 to identify this mineral.

Assess Performance

Obtain one or more samples of minerals from your teacher. Perform the tests needed to identify your samples. Refer to the "Properties of Minerals" table as you collect your data.

Problem Solving

1. You are about to take a mineral-collecting field trip. You plan to identify all the minerals you collect. List the materials you will need to take with you and explain what mineral property each material will be used to identify.

2. Compare the importance of quartz and iron to modern civilizations.

3. What might happen if, from now on, all mineral resources found and used were recycled?

CHAPTER 2

ROCKS

Rocks are made of minerals, and you find rocks of all kinds and sizes everywhere! They range from the sandstone pebble in a city park to the gigantic granite face of a cliff. Most rocks appear sturdy and unchanging. Actually, however, natural processes are constantly changing rocks. People too can transform rocks.

On the Cutting Edge

Edward Torres of Seaside Heights, New Jersey, is a stonecutter. He skillfully turns sheets of white, black, beige, red, or green marble into custom-made items. He crafts such things as fireplace mantels and counter tops.

A typical job for Torres begins when his material is delivered. A 5-ft by 8-ft sheet of 3/4 in.-thick marble, weighing 600 lb, is gently deposited onto his worktable by a forklift! Torres then uses a circular, diamond-toothed, wet saw to precisely cut the hard stone to the proper measurements. (Water cools the saw blade.) The fully processed piece, completed and polished, is a beautiful and useful item.

What *natural* processes change some materials into marble, or into other kinds of rocks, in the first place? What properties distinguish one kind of rock from another? In this chapter you'll explore these and other questions.

Coming Up

◀ Edward Torres, Stonecutter

HOW ARE ROCKS CLASSIFIED?

Rocks are the "stuff" that makes up Earth. About 4 billion years ago, Earth was a molten ball of rock. Although some of Earth's rock is still molten, the rock in the outer layer is solid. You live on this rocky ball. In this investigation you'll find out how rocks are identified and classified.

Activity
Sort of Rocky

Rocks are made of minerals. Some rocks are made of only one mineral, but most rocks are made of more than one. In this activity you'll observe some properties of rocks and use those properties to classify the rocks.

MATERIALS
- paper punchouts
- marker
- white glue
- set of rocks
- hand lens
- egg carton
- *Science Notebook*

Procedure

1. Number paper punchouts from 1 to 12. With white glue, glue one punchout on each rock specimen.

2. Put all the rocks together on your desktop. **Compare** the rocks to one another and separate them into a dark-colored set and a light-colored set. In your *Science Notebook*, **record** the numbers for each set.

3. Mineral crystals in rocks are usually very small. They are shiny and have flat faces that look like tiny mirrors. Place all the rocks together, **observe** the

rocks with a hand lens, and separate the rocks into a set with crystals and a set without crystals. **Record** the numbers for each set.

4. Use the hand lens to study the rocks again, separating the rocks into two new sets: one set in which the rocks appear to be made of more than one mineral and the other in which the rocks appear to contain only one mineral. **Record** the numbers for each set.

5. Separate the rocks with one mineral into two sets: rocks with crystals and rocks without crystals. Do the same for rocks with more than one mineral. **Record** your results.

6. Now **classify** each of the four sets from steps 4 and 5 into sets that contain dark-colored rocks and light-colored rocks. Then use the egg carton to store your rock specimens.

Analyze and Conclude

1. How many sets now contain only one rock?

2. List the properties that you used in this activity to classify rocks. **Infer** how these properties are used to classify rocks.

UNIT PROJECT LINK

Begin a rock collection. Rocks are easier to find than minerals. Get good clean rocks that are freshly broken so that you can see what the insides look like. Keep a numbered list of your rocks to tell where they came from. Try sorting them according to their properties.

Activity
The Rock Key

A key is used in science to help identify something. The Rock Key will help you use the properties of rocks to find out their names.

MATERIALS
- goggles
- rock set
- square glass plate
- hand lens
- *Science Notebook*

SAFETY //////
Wear goggles during this activity. When using the glass plate, hold it firmly on the table. Press a point of the rock against the plate and pull the rock toward you. DO NOT HOLD THE GLASS PLATE IN YOUR HAND.

Procedure

1. Choose a rock specimen. Look at the descriptions at the left side of the Rock Key. Which description matches your rock? Does it have crystals? If it does, follow the line from "Rock has crystals" to the next level in the key. If it does not have crystals, follow the other line.

2. At most levels in the key, two choices are given. Match a choice to your rock and follow the line to your next observation and choice. Eventually, you will arrive at the name of your rock on the right side of the key. Be sure to follow the lines in the key; don't skip around.

3. If you need to find out whether the rock is hard or soft, test the hardness against glass, the same as you did with minerals. Hard rocks scratch glass; soft ones do not.

4. If you need to find out if a rock with crystals is coarse-grained, medium-grained, or fine-grained, look at the size of crystals. In a coarse-grained rock, most of the rock is made of crystals larger than a grain of rice. In a fine-grained rock, you need a hand lens to see crystals. In a medium-grained rock, you can see the crystals without a hand lens, but they are smaller than rice grains.

Steps 3 & 4

Analyze and Conclude

1. Use the Rock Key to identify each of your rocks. For each rock, **record** in your *Science Notebook* the rock's number, its properties, and its name.

2. Which rocks did you find hard to identify? **Make an inference** about what additional data would have helped you identify them more easily.

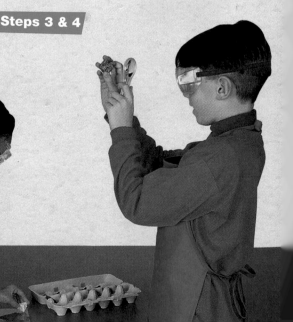

THE ROCK KEY

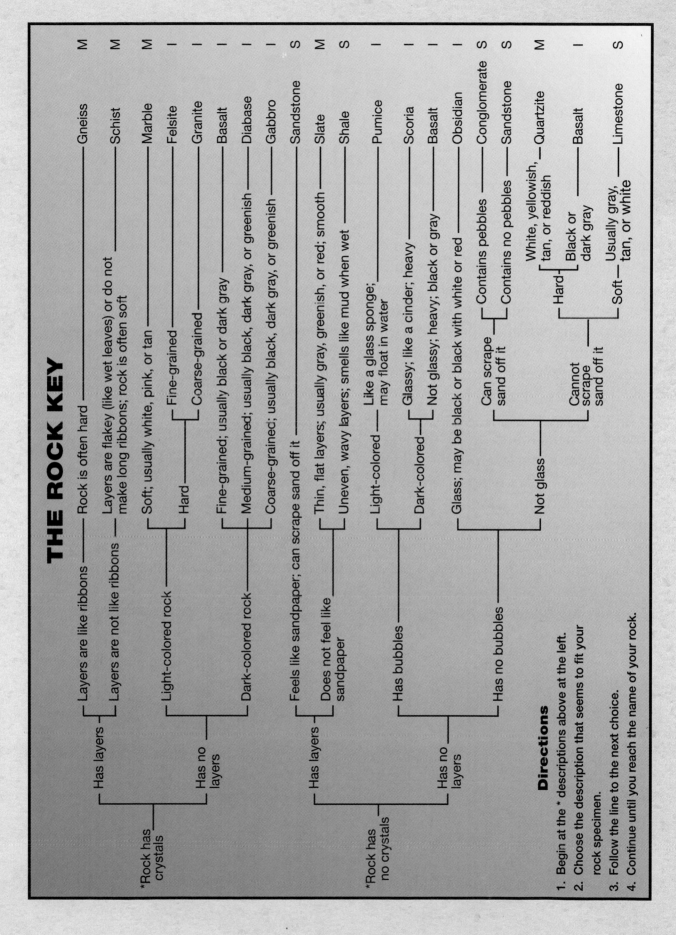

*Rock has crystals

- Has layers
  - Layers are like ribbons —— Rock is often hard —————————— Gneiss — M
  - Layers are not like ribbons —— Layers are flakey (like wet leaves) or do not make long ribbons; rock is often soft —— Schist — M
- Has no layers
  - Light-colored rock
    - Soft; usually white, pink, or tan ——————————— Marble — M
    - Hard
      - Fine-grained ————————————————— Felsite — I
      - Coarse-grained ———————————————— Granite — I
  - Dark-colored rock
    - Fine-grained; usually black or dark gray ——————— Basalt — I
    - Medium-grained; usually black, dark gray, or greenish — Diabase — I
    - Coarse-grained; usually black, dark gray, or greenish — Gabbro — I

*Rock has no crystals

- Has layers
  - Feels like sandpaper; can scrape sand off it ——————————— Sandstone — S
  - Does not feel like sandpaper
    - Thin, flat layers; usually gray, greenish, or red; smooth ——— Slate — M
    - Uneven, wavy layers; smells like mud when wet —————— Shale — S
- Has no layers
  - Has bubbles
    - Light-colored —— Like a glass sponge; may float in water ——— Pumice — I
    - Dark-colored
      - Glassy; like a cinder; heavy ————————————— Scoria — I
      - Not glassy; heavy; black or gray ————————— Basalt — I
  - Has no bubbles
    - Glass; may be black or black with white or red —————————— Obsidian — I
    - Not glass
      - Can scrape sand off it
        - Contains pebbles ——————————————— Conglomerate — S
        - Contains no pebbles —————————————— Sandstone — S
      - Cannot scrape sand off it
        - Hard
          - White, yellowish, tan, or reddish ——————— Quartzite — M
          - Black or dark gray ——————————————— Basalt — I
        - Soft — Usually gray, tan, or white ——————————— Limestone — S

Directions

1. Begin at the * descriptions above at the left.
2. Choose the description that seems to fit your rock specimen.
3. Follow the line to the next choice.
4. Continue until you reach the name of your rock.

Igneous Rocks:
A Hot Item

Rocks are made of minerals. In the activities, you grouped rocks based on how they were similar and different. Scientists, too, place rocks into groups. But they group them as to how they formed. This classification system includes three types of rocks. Let's take a close look at one of those types, called igneous (ig'nē əs) rocks.

Igneous rocks are probably the most common rocks found on Earth. The word *igneous* comes from the Latin word for "fire." Knowing this, can you guess how igneous rocks form? **Igneous rocks** form when hot, melted rock material cools and hardens. Rock that is melted to a liquid form is called molten rock. Where on Earth do you think molten rock is found?

Igneous Rocks From Magma

Deep within Earth, the temperature is much hotter than it is near the surface. Rocks melt, or change from solids to liquids. This molten rock material that forms deep within Earth is called **magma**. Because it is less dense than the material around it, magma tends to slowly rise toward the surface. As magma rises, it sometimes cools and hardens before reaching the surface.

Because it is below the surface, magma cools very slowly. As it cools, mineral grains, or crystals, have a long time to form. So the mineral grains are large in rocks formed from magma. Which rocks in your collection do you think formed from magma?

One of the most common rocks

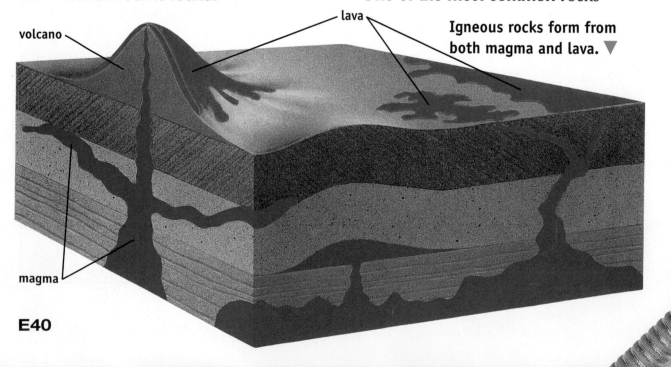

volcano

lava

magma

Igneous rocks form from both magma and lava. ▼

E40

formed from magma is granite, which is shown below. Notice that it consists of different minerals. The pink-colored and gray-colored mineral is feldspar, the white mineral is quartz, and the black mineral is mica. Notice the size of the mineral grains that make up granite. Have you seen granite in use around your community? If so, how was this rock used?

Stone Mountain, which towers high above the surrounding land in the state of Georgia, is a mountain of granite. Where did this rock harden? How do you think this rock became exposed at Earth's surface?

Not all the igneous rocks that harden from magma are the same. They vary in the kinds of mineral grains that form. The kinds of minerals that form depend on the composition of the magma.

Gabbro is another kind of igneous rock. Like all rocks that cool from magma, it has large mineral grains. But notice that gabbro is mostly made of dark-colored minerals, in this case pyroxene (pī raks'ēn) and olivine. It has few light-colored minerals, such as quartz.

▲ **Stone Mountain in Georgia**

Igneous Rocks From Lava

You know that magma rises toward Earth's surface. What do you think might happen when it breaks through to the surface? Magma that reaches Earth's surface is called **lava**. Look back at the diagram showing lava and magma on page E40. An opening in Earth's surface through which lava flows is called a volcano. When lava cools and hardens at Earth's surface, it also forms igneous rock.

Three kinds of rocks that formed from lava are shown on page E42. Compare them with the photograph of granite. How do the sizes of the mineral grains compare? Use what you have learned about igneous rocks to explain why the grains differ in size.

▼ **Granite**

Gabbro ▶

E41

▲ Basalt   ▲ Obsidian   Rhyolite ▶

Basalt is an igneous rock that forms when lava rich in dark-colored minerals cools and hardens. Find *basalt* on the chart below and note that its composition is similar to that of gabbro. Because it flows out onto Earth's surface, lava cools faster than magma. So rocks cooled from lava, such as basalt, have smaller grains than rocks cooled from magma, such as gabbro. Large areas of the states of Washington and Oregon are covered by basalt, because of past volcanic activity.

Obsidian (əb sid'ē ən) is another igneous rock, often called natural glass. Lava that forms obsidian cools and hardens so quickly that mineral grains have very little time to grow. This rapid cooling gives the rock its glassy look.

Native Americans once used obsidian to make cutting tools such as blades, because obsidian forms sharp edges when broken.

Look at the photograph of the igneous rock rhyolite (rī'ə līt). Find it on the chart. How do you think rhyolite forms? ■

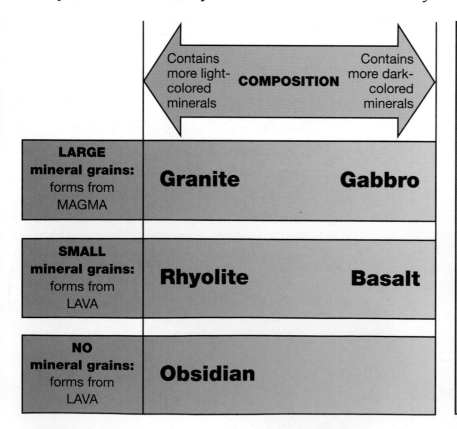

	Contains more light-colored minerals ◀ COMPOSITION ▶ Contains more dark-colored minerals	
LARGE mineral grains: forms from MAGMA	**Granite**	**Gabbro**
SMALL mineral grains: forms from LAVA	**Rhyolite**	**Basalt**
NO mineral grains: forms from LAVA	**Obsidian**	

INVESTIGATE FURTHER!

EXPERIMENT

Work with a partner to make a model that shows how igneous rocks form. Make "magma" by dissolving as much salt or sugar as possible in very little hot water. Cool half the magma very slowly at room temperature. Cool the other half quickly in a refrigerator. Which magma produced larger "minerals"? Why?

Sedimentary Rocks:
Rocks From Pieces

Sedimentary (sed ə men'tər ē) **rocks** are rocks that form at Earth's surface when sediments harden into rock. **Sediments** include bits of existing rocks, minerals, and organic materials. (Remember that things that are called organic were once living.)

There are many different kinds of sedimentary rocks. In fact, you probably use one sedimentary rock every day in school. Can you guess which sedimentary rock is used by students and teachers in the classroom? You also may have used it to draw on the sidewalk. Chalk is a sedimentary rock.

Animal, Vegetable, or Mineral?

Just like igneous rocks, sedimentary rocks can be grouped according to how they form. There are three types of sedimentary rocks: clastic, chemical, and organic. Clastic sedimentary rocks are those in which pieces of rocks, minerals, and organic materials are cemented together. The bits of sediment that make up clastic rocks can be as small as single grains of mud or as large as boulders! As you might expect, sedimentary rocks are common on Earth's surface.

Clastic rocks are grouped according to the size of the sediments they contain. Conglomerate (kən gläm'ər it), shale, and sandstone are examples of clastic rocks. Study the photos of these rocks. How do their sediment pieces compare?

Most clastic rocks form when wind, water, or ice carry and then drop sediments. Over time, these materials

◀ Conglomerate

Sandstone ▶

▲ Shale

become compacted, or squeezed together. Minerals dissolved in water seep into spaces between the materials. As the water dries and the minerals grow, the minerals bind the loose sediments into solid rock. This binding of sediments is called **cementation** (sē men tā'shən).

Sandstone, as you might have guessed, is made of small, sand-sized rock bits. Sandstone often feels gritty, like sandpaper. Where on Earth do you think sandstone might be forming? Can you think of any uses for sandstone?

Chemical sedimentary rocks form when water rich in dissolved minerals evaporates, leaving the minerals behind, or when chemical changes form new minerals. Rock gypsum, rock salt, and some kinds of limestone are examples of chemical sedimentary rocks.

The type of limestone shown in the photograph below consists mostly of calcite, which formed when sea or lake waters evaporated. Limestone is ground and mixed with other ingredients to make certain cements.

▲ **Rock gypsum**

Rock gypsum forms when water evaporates, leaving behind the mineral gypsum. Gypsum is used in plaster of Paris and plaster walls.

Rock salt, which is almost pure halite, is known to you as table salt. It does, however, have other uses, as you can see in the photo below.

▼ **Limestone**

▲ **Rock salt is commonly used to melt ice and snow.**

The third type of sedimentary rock is called organic rock. Organic rocks form from the remains of plants and animals or from parts, such as shells, of organisms. One type of coal is an organic sedimentary rock that forms when bits of dead plants are compacted over long periods of time. The squeezing removes all the water, leaving behind the carbon that forms coal.

Limestone forms in different ways. Some limestones form when shells of dead sea animals become cemented together. Limestone consists mostly of calcite. Fine-grained limestones, such as chalk, form when calcite comes in contact with acid.

Features of Sedimentary Rocks

Scientists, including budding scientists like you, can learn about how a sedimentary rock was formed by observing the features preserved in the rock. When sediments are dropped by water, wind, or ice, the sediments build up in layers. A layer can be as thin as a sheet of paper or as thick as a few meters! The layers harden over time. And as more sediments are dropped, more layers are formed. So most sedimentary rocks are layered. This layering is often called bedding. Wind, water, and the shape of the land can all affect the formation of beds of sedimentary rock. Use the chart on page E46 to compare how sediment beds form.

SCIENCE IN LITERATURE

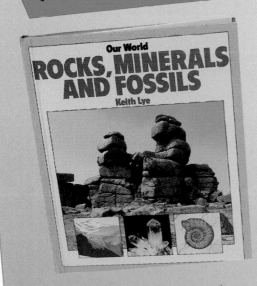

ROCKS, MINERALS AND FOSSILS
by Keith Lye
Silver Burdett Press, 1991

The sedimentary rocks of the Grand Canyon of the Colorado River are more than amazing scenery. The canyon is also a 3-D lesson on the history of Earth! Find out how to "read the rocks" on pages 32 and 33 of *Rocks, Minerals and Fossils*.

Then turn to pages 34 and 35 to see what creatures lived when each of the rock layers of the Grand Canyon formed. These fossils help scientists to read the history of life on Earth.

Sediment Beds

◀ Notice that the surface of this sediment layer looks wavy. These wavy lines are called ripple marks. They are formed by moving water or wind. You may have seen ripple marks near a stream or on a beach. How might they become sedimentary rock?

◀ Most sediment beds, like these in shale, were deposited horizontally, resulting in the characteristic layering of sedimentary rock.

◀ The beds in this sandstone show cross-bedding. They formed when wind dropped sand on the curved slopes of sand dunes. Eventually, the sand beds hardened to form sandstone. What kinds of places can you think of that have sand dunes?

◀ Mud cracks are another feature sometimes preserved in sedimentary rocks. Mud cracks are evidence of wet periods followed by dry periods during the formation of a rock.

If you've ever gone rock collecting or to a natural history museum, you've probably seen fossils. A **fossil** is any remains or evidence of an organism from the past. Sedimentary rocks sometimes contain fossils. The photograph shows a fossil fern. Based on this fossil, what conclusions might you draw about how this rock formed?

Refer to the Rock Key and the rocks that you identified in the activity on page E38. Which rocks in your collection are sedimentary rocks? (The Rock Key uses a letter S to show them.) Try to classify the sedimentary rocks in your collection as clastic, chemical, or organic, based on their properties. ■

Fossil fern ▶

Metamorphic Rocks:
A Change of Identity

The third major group of rocks is the metamorphic (met ə môr′fik) rocks. The word *metamorphic* is made of two word parts that mean "to change form." In some ways, metamorphic rocks are like sedimentary rocks because both kinds form from existing rocks. In other ways, metamorphic rocks are like igneous rocks because both kinds can form at high temperatures and pressures. So what qualities make metamorphic rocks different from both sedimentary and igneous rocks? Let's find out.

New Rocks

Metamorphic rocks are new rocks that form from existing rocks because of changes caused by heat, pressure, or chemicals. The existing rocks that are changed may be sedimentary, igneous, or other metamorphic rocks. The change from one rock type to another is called metamorphism.

Some changes that occur with metamorphism result in changes in texture. *Texture* refers to the size and shape of mineral grains and the way in which they are arranged in a rock. In other cases, changes in composition, or makeup, take place. The changes that occur during metamorphism can result from three different sets of conditions.

Contact metamorphism occurs when hot magma or lava comes in contact with rock. The rock gets "baked" by the molten

Metamorphic rocks form when existing rocks are changed by heat, pressure, and chemicals. ▼

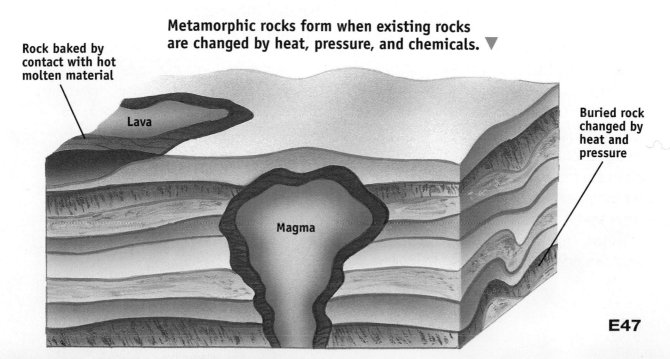

Rock baked by contact with hot molten material

Lava

Magma

Buried rock changed by heat and pressure

material. So temperature alone, not pressure, causes the rock to change. Changes can occur in the kinds of minerals present and in the sizes of the grains. Liquids and gases escaping from the magma can also chemically change minerals in the surrounding rocks.

A second type of metamorphism is called regional metamorphism. It occurs in rocks that are buried deep below the surface, where temperature and pressure are high. The texture of the rocks changes, particularly in the way the minerals are arranged. Mineral grains tend to become lined up in the same direction because of high pressures. Also, high temperatures cause changes in the original mineral composition of the rocks.

Burial metamorphism causes the least amount of change in a rock. Burial metamorphism occurs when the weight of rocks and sediments burying a rock puts pressure on that rock. During burial metamorphism, the temperatures and pressures involved are low compared with those of other kinds of metamorphism. Low temperatures and pressures, for example, can cause new minerals to grow and textures to change slightly. Such changes cause

shale, a sedimentary rock, to become the metamorphic rock called slate.

Banded Metamorphic Rocks

Metamorphic rocks are grouped according to their textures as banded or nonbanded. As you would expect, rocks with a banded texture look as if they contain bands, or thin layers, which may look wavy or straight. You are probably familiar with some banded metamorphic rocks. Gneiss (nīs) is a banded metamorphic rock that contains quartz, mica, and feldspar. Which igneous rock is made of these same three minerals? Look at the photograph of gneiss. Note the bands of mineral grains. In which direction do you think the pressure was applied during metamorphism?

Another banded metamorphic rock is slate. Recall that slate forms when shale, a sedimentary rock, is exposed to changes in temperature and pressure. Slate is used as a roofing material. Some chalkboards are even made of slate. When exposed to more heat and pressure, slate can become another banded metamorphic rock, called phyllite (fil'īt).

▼ **Gneiss**

Phyllite ▶

Slate ▶

E48

▲ Marble

▲ Quartzite

Nonbanded Metamorphic Rocks

In nonbanded metamorphic rocks the mineral grains have not been lined up by pressure. The texture of these rocks is described as massive. Look at the photographs of the nonbanded rocks above. Contrast them with the photographs of banded rocks. Can you infer the meaning of the term *massive* as used to describe metamorphic rocks?

Marble is a nonbanded metamorphic rock. Marble forms when limestone is changed by metamorphism. Marble can be white, black, pink, gray, or green with streaks of other colors.

Another nonbanded metamorphic rock is quartzite (kwôrts′īt). Quartzite forms when quartz-rich sandstone is exposed to high pressures and temperatures. ■

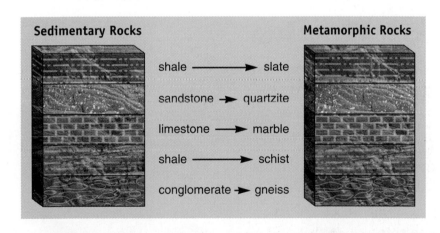

Sedimentary Rocks   **Metamorphic Rocks**

shale ——→ slate

sandstone ─→ quartzite

limestone ——→ marble

shale ——→ schist

conglomerate ─→ gneiss

◄ **The drawing shows the different parent rocks of metamorphic rocks. Try to match metamorphic rocks in your collection with their parent rocks.**

INVESTIGATION 1

THINK IT WRITE IT

1. Name the three basic types of rocks and describe how each formed.

2. Fossils are found almost exclusively in sedimentary rocks. Suggest a hypothesis to explain this observation.

How Do the Properties of Rocks Make Them Useful?

Make a rock! Punch small holes in the bottom of a paper cup. Pour a handful of sand into the cup. Dilute some white glue with a little water. Pour it into the sand. Let the water drain out. After it has dried, tear off the paper and behold your "rock." What are its properties? Find a use for it!

Activity

Comparing Properties of Rocks

Different kinds of rocks have different properties, which make the rocks useful in different ways.

MATERIALS

- rock set
- hand lens
- *Science Notebook*

Procedure

1. Look at the Rock Key on page E39. The column at the far right lists the letters *I, S,* and *M*. These stand for igneous, sedimentary, and metamorphic.

2. Separate your rocks into three sets so that the first set has all the rocks labeled *I* on the Rock Key, the second set contains those labeled *S*, and the third, those labeled *M*.

3. **Predict** which sets will have layered rocks. Look for layered rocks and **record** your observations in your *Science Notebook*.

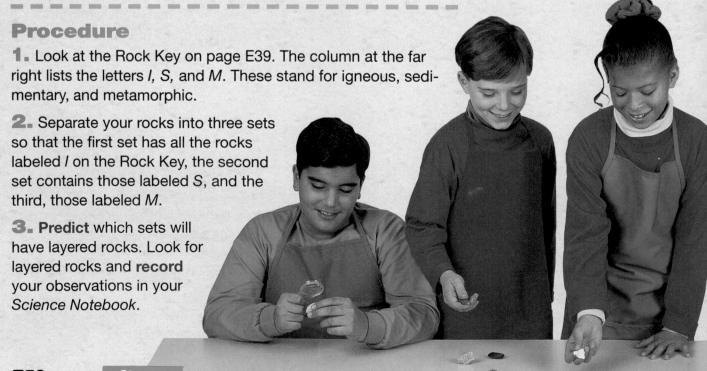

4. **Predict** which sets will have crystalline rocks (rocks with crystals). Look for crystalline rocks and **record** your observations.

5. **Predict** which rocks will be made of particles or fragments. Look for rocks that are made of particles or fragments. **Record** your observations.

6. **Compare and contrast** the rocks in your collection. **Record** as many properties as you can for each rock.

Analyze and Conclude

1. In which group(s) of rocks do you find layers, and in which do you not find layers?

2. In which group(s) of rocks do you find crystals, and in which do you not find crystals?

3. In which group(s) do you find particles or fragments, and in which do you not find particles or fragments?

4. Consider the properties of the rocks in your collection. Then make **inferences** about some uses for the rocks.

INVESTIGATE FURTHER!

RESEARCH

How's your rock collection coming? Do some research to find out how the types of rocks in your collection are used by people.

Rock Quarries

Have you ever seen a fireplace built of rocks? How about a rock wall or a path lined with stones? Chances are, the rocks that make up these things came from a quarry (kwôr′ē). A rock **quarry** is a mine, usually close to or at Earth's surface, from which certain rocks are removed. Billions of tons of granite, sandstone, limestone, slate, marble, and other types of rocks are removed each year from quarries all over the world.

Rock is removed from quarries in two forms. Dimension stones are slabs of rock that are removed from quarries in specific shapes and sizes. Most dimension stones are used to build things that will both last and look decorative, such as buildings. So the slabs must be solid and have an attractive texture, pattern, or color.

Most of the rock removed from quarries is in another form, called crushed stone. Crushed stone consists of bits and pieces of rocks that are primarily used in concrete, cements, and other construction materials.

You've probably tried to break or move a few big rocks at times. It isn't easy. So how do you suppose rocks are mined in quarries? How rocks are mined depends on how they'll be used. Most crushed stone gets blasted from solid rock with the use of explosives. First, holes are drilled into the rock. Then explosives are placed in the holes

Marble being cut at a quarry ▼

Marble slab being lifted by crane ▼

Transporting marble slabs ▼

and set off, causing the rock to break up. Of course, this wouldn't be a great way to quarry dimension stones, unless you are planning to cement the pieces back together!

In most quarries, dimension stones are cut from solid rock by using either a drill or a torch. Air moving through the drill makes the drill bit, or tip, spin rapidly. As it spins, the bit cuts away at the rock. A torch, on the other hand, cuts the rock by melting it. When cut with a torch, the edges of the slabs are smooth.

Once the dimension stones are cut, a huge crane is used to move them. The blocks of rock, which can weigh several tons each, are secured with hooks and chains. Then the crane is used to slowly lift and carry the stones.

From the quarry, loose slabs are transported to a processing mill. Many quarries that mine dimension stones have their own processing mills. At these mills, the rock slabs are cut to certain sizes by using steel wires and rock saws. The saw blades are often made with diamonds. As you learned in Chapter 1, diamonds are the hardest known minerals. They can cut through even the hardest rocks with the greatest of ease.

Once the rocks are cut and sized, they may be polished. Polishing gradually smooths out any wire or saw marks left from the cutting stage. When the dimension stones are highly polished, they are ready to be shipped around the corner, around the country, or around the world. The chart shows some common dimension stones, where they come from, and what they are used for. Do any quarried rocks come from your state? What states might produce the marble for a counter top? Which stones might be used in monuments? ■

Rock	Where From	Uses
Granite	Vermont, Massachusetts, Maine, New Hampshire, Rhode Island, Minnesota, Wisconsin	monuments, buildings, grave markers
Sandstone	New York, Ohio, Pennsylvania, Kentucky, Connecticut	buildings, trim
Marble	Vermont, Georgia	monuments, buildings, flooring, counter tops, kitchen items
Limestone	Texas, Utah, Indiana, Missouri, Florida, Minnesota	decorative trims, buildings, monuments, park benches

A Ton of Bricks!

HOW IT Works

Is your home or school made of bricks? Do you think bricks are rocks? Although they are hard like most rocks and are made from minerals, bricks aren't actually rocks. "Well, why not?" you may be asking yourself. Rocks are made of one or more minerals, and they form naturally. Since rocks are formed by nature,

bricks cannot be rocks because bricks are made by people!

Brick Making Today

What, then, *are* bricks? Bricks are small, rectangular blocks made from a mixture of clays and other sediments. To make bricks, different kinds and amounts of clays are dug from river bottoms or other places on Earth's surface.

To make bricks, clays and sediments are removed from Earth, ground into powder, mixed with water to form a paste, poured into molds, and hardened by baking in kilns. ▼

These minerals are taken to a factory where they are crushed into a fine powder. Sometimes the powder is sifted to remove any large pieces. Water is added to the powder to make a thick, gooey paste. The paste is pressed into molds that are coated with sand or water. The coating helps to prevent the mixture from sticking to the molds, much as butter helps to keep cake batter from sticking to a pan.

Next, molds are placed in a kiln, or drying oven. When the clay mixture is completely dry, the molds are fired in another kiln. Firing chemically changes the clay blocks by heating them for up to 12 hours at temperatures above 800°C (1,500°F). Once fired, the bricks are cooled and taken to other parts of the factory to be packed and shipped.

Brick Making in the Past

Scientists who study ancient cultures discovered that bricks have been used by people for at least 60 centuries! The first bricks were probably simple mud blocks dried in the sun. Adobe (ə dō′bē), or sun-dried brick, is thought to have first been made in dry areas of the world, including parts of Africa, Spain, Peru, and the southwestern part of the United States. Adobe bricks are made with a mixture of clay, sand, and sometimes, straw. The materials are mixed by hand, with bare feet, or with a simple tool. The mixture is then put into molds and allowed to dry for at least two weeks. When dry, the bricks are removed from the molds and used.

About 3,500 years ago, people began to fire bricks. They discovered that firing the clay blocks made them harder and longer-lasting.

Bricks are not rocks. But like sedimentary rocks, bricks are made of sediments. Also, with firing, clay is changed chemically to a different material. How is this similar to the way some metamorphic rocks form? ■

▲ **This structure is made from adobe brick.**

INVESTIGATION 2

1. Identify some ways in which rocks differ.

2. Suppose you were asked to recommend a type of rock that could be used to make a strong but attractive building. Use the Rock Key for help in making your suggestion. Give reasons to support your choice.

HOW DO ROCKS CHANGE OVER TIME?

It may seem that rocks last forever, but they don't. They change, just like everything else. Unwrap some broken crayons and set them on wax paper in the hot sun. What happens? What rock-forming change have you just modeled?

Activity

'Round and 'Round She Goes

It may take hundreds of thousands of years, even millions of years, but Earth materials go through changes called the rock cycle. In this activity you'll investigate this cycle.

MATERIALS
- rock cycle diagram
- rock set
- vial of sand
- vial of clay
- seashell
- *Science Notebook*

Procedure

1. Place the rock cycle diagram on your desktop.

2. Granite, sandstone, sand, and quartzite form part of a loop in the rock cycle. Use those samples from your rock set and **make a model** of the rock cycle by placing the sand and rocks in their correct places on the rock cycle. Then, in your *Science Notebook*, **draw** the part of the loop they make. Label your drawing to show the kinds of materials or rocks and the processes these go through in changing from one to another.

3. Gneiss, sandstone, and sand make a complete loop in the rock cycle. Use those samples and put them in order on the rock cycle. **Draw** and label this loop.

4. Basalt, slate, shale, and clay make another part of a loop. Use your samples and put these in order on the rock cycle. **Draw** and label this loop.

5. Another part of a loop in the rock cycle is made by seashells, marble, and limestone. Get samples of these materials and include them on your rock cycle. **Draw** and label this loop.

Step 2

Analyze and Conclude

1. Explain why the loop in step 3 is a complete cycle that could happen over and over again.

2. In step 2, why don't the materials listed form a complete loop? What is missing to make this loop a complete cycle of the rock cycle?

3. **Suggest a definition** of the rock cycle, based on how you think it works.

INVESTIGATE FURTHER!

EXPERIMENT

Think of another complete loop in the rock cycle, a loop formed by materials you already have or can obtain. Place samples on your copy of the rock cycle; then draw and label your loop.

Coal:
A Fossil Fuel

How might you describe coal to someone who has never seen it or who knows nothing about it? You might explain that one kind of coal is a sedimentary rock and one kind is a metamorphic rock. You might also say that coal can be burned to heat your home. Would you describe coal as a fossil fuel?

As you might suspect from its name, a fossil fuel is a material formed from plant or animal remains that can be burned for energy. Over millions of years, pressures and temperatures have squeezed and changed the remains. Left behind are elements, such as carbon, hydrogen, and oxygen, that once made up the organisms. Coal is one kind of fossil fuel.

Millions of years ago

PEAT
60% Carbon

Coal begins to form when swamp plants die and are quickly buried beneath sediments and other plants. Tiny organisms called bacteria cause organic material to decay and change. Over time, a dark, watery organic material called peat forms.

Peat Layer

LIGNITE
70% Carbon

With time, the peat gets buried by more sediments. The weight of these sediments compacts the peat and squeezes water out. Eventually, the percent of carbon present increases and a sedimentary rock called lignite, a type of coal, forms.

Lignite Layer

All forms of coal are used as fuel. Coal is burned to provide energy to heat homes, offices, and other buildings. Some coal is used to fuel furnaces in factories. In fact, coal provides about 20 percent of the energy needs in the United States.

Bituminous (bi tōō'mə nəs) coal lights very easily and provides the most energy of all the types of coal. But burning this kind of coal produces a sooty residue and yellow smoke. Anthracite (an'thrə sīt) coal burns much cleaner and longer than bituminous coal, but does not provide as much energy. The diagram below shows the changes coal can go through. ■

Peat ▼

Lignite ▼

▲ Bituminous Coal

▲ Anthracite

Present Day

BITUMINOUS COAL
80% Carbon
As the rock becomes buried deeper, temperature and pressure increase. Nearly all of the water that was once in the plant parts gets forced out and bituminous coal forms. Recall that bituminous coal, or soft coal, is a sedimentary rock that is mostly carbon.

Bituminous Layer

ANTHRACITE
95% Carbon
With deep burying and great temperature and pressure, bituminous coal becomes metamorphosed to form anthracite. Anthracite is a metamorphic rock. It has the highest percent of carbon of all the forms of coal.

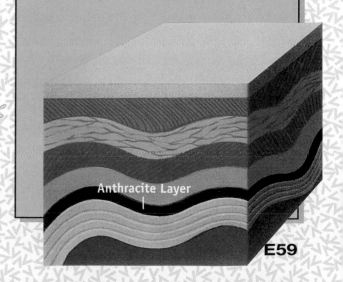

Anthracite Layer

E59

Rocks in Circles

 You learned that high temperatures and great pressures can change any rock into a metamorphic rock. But did you realize that any kind of rock—igneous, sedimentary, or metamorphic—can be changed into another kind of rock, not just by metamorphism?

Melting and cooling are just two of Earth's agents of change. They act to change Earth's rock materials. The series of changes that rocks undergo is called the **rock cycle**.

Notice the ovals in the diagram of the rock cycle. They represent five kinds of rock materials: igneous rock, sedimentary rock, metamorphic rock, sediments, and molten rock (magma and lava). Between the ovals are things that cause rock materials to change—factors such as melting and pressure. When you play most board games, you can move in only one direction around the board. But with the rock cycle, rocks may "move," or change, in many ways. To use the diagram to see how one type of rock changes into another, start at any oval. Then move in the direction of any arrow coming out of the oval. Follow the arrows, and you can't go wrong.

Sedimentary to Metamorphic

As you can see from the diagram, there are many factors in the rock cycle that cause change. Find the words *Sedimentary Rock* on the diagram. What's one way in which sedimentary rock can change? You know that sedimentary rocks form at or near Earth's surface. What do you think happens when these rocks become buried? High temperatures and pressures deep below the surface change sedimentary rocks into metamorphic rocks. Follow this change on the diagram.

Metamorphic to Igneous

Now what do you suppose happens when the pressures and temperatures deep below the surface become very high? Melting, or the changing of a solid to a liquid, occurs to change metamorphic rock into molten rock. Find *Melting* on the diagram.

As magma or lava cools, minerals form. When minerals form, they grow into different-sized crystals, so this step is sometimes called crystallizing. Notice in the rock cycle diagram that magma and lava cool and crystallize to form igneous rock. On the diagram, follow the change from metamorphic rock to igneous rock.

THE ROCK CYCLE

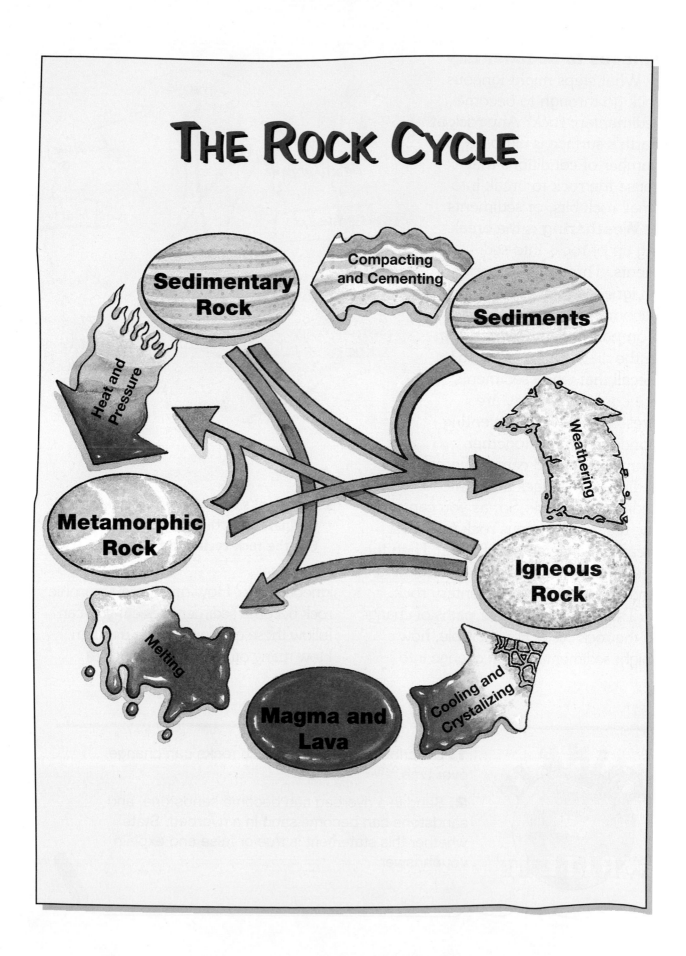

Igneous to Sedimentary

What steps might igneous rock go through to become sedimentary rock? Any rock at Earth's surface is exposed to a number of conditions that cause the rock to break into small rock bits, or sediments.

Weathering is the breaking up of rocks into sediments. Through weathering, an igneous rock can eventually become sediment bits. Find *Compacting* and *Cementing* in the diagram on page E61. Recall that when sediments are compacted, they are pressed together. Cementing bonds sediments together. Compacting and cementing of sediments changes them into sedimentary rock. So, as you can see in the diagram, igneous rock must first weather to become sediment. Then the sediment is compacted and cemented and changed into sedimentary rock.

There are many other paths of change in the rock cycle. For example, how might sedimentary rock change into

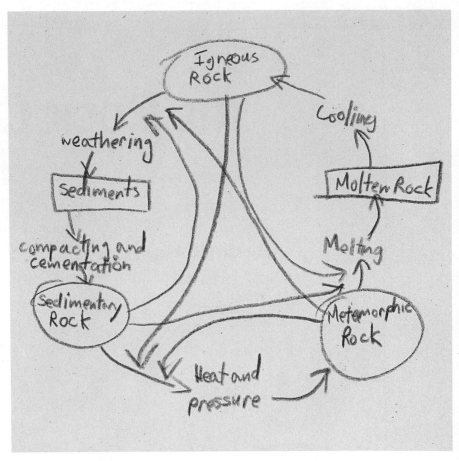

▲ A student's drawing of the rock cycle. Compare it to the diagram on page E61. Can the rock cycle start at any point?

igneous rock? How might metamorphic rock become sediment? See if you can follow these changes on the diagram. How many others can you find? ■

INVESTIGATION 3

1. Describe four ways by which rocks can change over time.

2. Sand in a riverbed can become sandstone, and sandstone can become sand in a riverbed. State whether this statement is true or false and explain your answer.

REFLECT & EVALUATE

WORD POWER

cementation   quarry
fossil   rock cycle
lava   rocks
magma   sediments
igneous rocks
metamorphic rocks
sedimentary rocks

👤 On Your Own

Review the terms in the list. Then use as many terms as you can in a paragraph about how rocks are related.

👥 With a Partner

Write a slogan for one of the terms. Do not use the term. (You may use other terms in the slogan.) Share the slogan with a group and have them guess the term.

BUILD YOUR PORTFOLIO

Write a story about the trip a rock material makes in one complete cycle through the rock cycle. Be sure to name all rock materials. Be creative, but base your fiction on scientific fact.

Analyze Information

Explain how the cycle shown could be never ending. Then describe an event that could break the cycle.

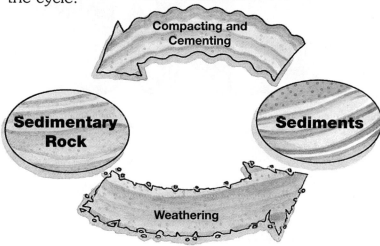

Assess Performance

Obtain several samples of unknown rock. Using a hand lens and the Rock Key on page E39, identify each sample and classify each as igneous, sedimentary, or metamorphic.

Problem Solving

1. You observe that a rock has large crystals and is unlayered. What type of rock would you infer it to be? Explain your inference.

2. How are the rock cycle and the yearly cycle of changing seasons alike and not alike?

3. Make a sketch that illustrates the rock cycle. Use examples of rocks from this chapter in your sketch.

EARTH'S STRUCTURES

Did you know that you can float with both feet on the ground? In fact, you're always floating—even when you think you're standing still. Here's why. The ground under your feet is drifting on a layer of hot, gooey rock. This rock is only one of the remarkable materials that make up Earth. Sometimes the drifting movement leads to earthquakes.

A Deep, Deep Quake

On June 8, 1994, an unusual earthquake struck the country of Bolivia, in South America. The quake was severe, but it caused relatively little damage and no loss of life because the quake was located very deep beneath Earth's surface. Such rare, deep earthquakes usually cause little damage. And they come with a bonus for seismologists (sīz mäl'ə jists), the scientists who study earthquakes. The vibrations caused by a deep quake provide much information about Earth's interior. By measuring the activity from the Bolivia quake at different locations around the world, scientists learned a great deal about the materials that make up the inner Earth. You might say that the scientists received a picture of the interior structure of our planet. What is inside Earth? What causes earthquakes? The investigations in this chapter will help you find out.

Coming Up

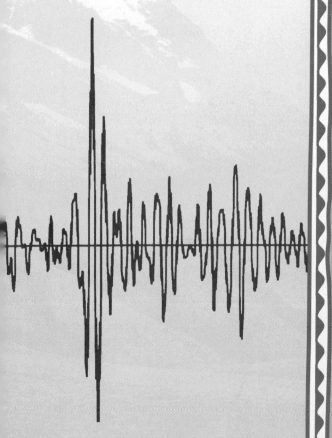

◀ A seismograph recording of the deep earthquake in Bolivia

WHAT IS EARTH'S STRUCTURE?

How do rocks make up the sphere you call Earth? What's at the center of that sphere? This investigation will help you answer such questions about Earth's structure by looking at what's inside as well as outside Earth.

Activity

A Model Earth

An apple makes a good model of Earth's structure. In science, a model is used to help us understand something else. Sometimes a model helps us to ask better questions. Let's look carefully at an apple.

MATERIALS
- apple
- plastic knife
- wax paper
- *Science Notebook*

Procedure

1. Place a piece of wax paper on your desktop. Put an apple on the wax paper.

2. Use the apple to **model** the interior of Earth. Cut the apple in half. Carefully **observe** the cut surface from the skin to the center of the apple. In your *Science Notebook*, **sketch** and **describe** what you see.

Step 2

3. Cut both halves in half again. The skin represents Earth's **crust,** or surface layer. The skin on three of the pieces is a model for the amount of Earth's crust that is covered by oceans.

4. Examine one of the pieces of apple carefully. **Compare** the thickness of the skin to the thickness of the rest of the piece.

Analyze and Conclude

1. Based on your model, how much of Earth's crust is covered by oceans? How much of the crust is land?

2. Earth has a layer below its crust called the **mantle.** The mantle covers a ball, called the **core**, in the middle of Earth. **Infer** which parts of the apple are models for the mantle and the core.

3. Compare the thicknesses of the crust, mantle, and core in your model. Based on your model, what conclusions can you draw about the depths, or thicknesses, of the layers of Earth?

Step 3

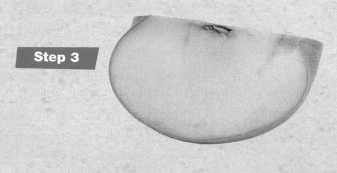

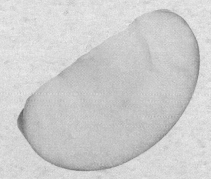

INVESTIGATE FURTHER!

RESEARCH

Earth's land includes mountains, plains, plateaus, and other types of landforms. Find out how much of Earth's surface is land on which people can plant crops. How much of the land is largely uninhabitable?

The Sphere We Live On

When you hear the word *model*, what do you think of? You may picture a model airplane or a fashion model. In science, a **model** is something used to represent an object or an idea. In the activity on pages E66 and E67, you used an apple as a model of Earth.

What would happen if you took a huge knife and sliced right through Earth instead of through an apple? You'd see four layers instead of three—so your model was a bit too simple. Now take a look at another Earth model, the diagram shown here.

The Crust

Earth's outer layer is called the **crust**. It is the thinnest of all the layers, but it varies in thickness around Earth. It can be as thin as 10 km (6 mi) under the oceans and as thick as 65 km (40 mi) below the continents.

The crust is made up of solid rock. It is mostly granite, gabbro, and basalt, but it also includes all the igneous, sedimentary, and metamorphic rocks you have learned about. Much of the crust is covered by oceans, lakes, rivers, sediments, plants, and soil.

Earth has four layers. ▼

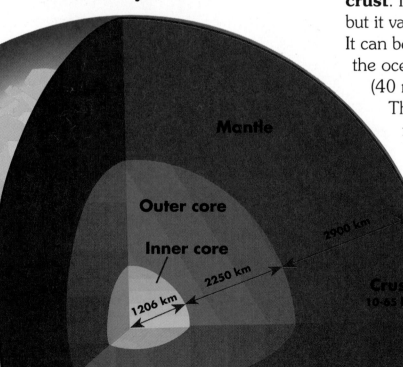

Mantle

Outer core

Inner core

1206 km

2250 km

2900 km

Crust
10–65 km

The crust is broken into many large and small pieces called plates. These plates float like rafts on the layer below the crust. So they can move very slowly around Earth's surface, carrying the continents and oceans with them.

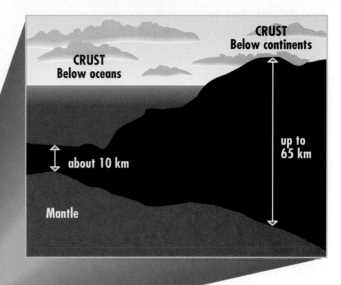

Earth's crust is thicker beneath continents than beneath oceans. ▼

CRUST
Below oceans

CRUST
Below continents

about 10 km

up to 65 km

Mantle

Crust
Mantle
Outer core
Inner core

The Mantle

Below the crust is the **mantle**. It is the thickest layer, taking up about 84 percent of Earth's volume. The part of this layer that is closest to the crust is made of solid rock that has the same properties as other solids. However, much of the mantle is solid rock that has some properties of liquids. It can flow like maple syrup or be stretched out like putty.

Much of the mantle is composed of an igneous rock called peridotite. This rock is dark in color and rich in the elements iron, magnesium, and silicon.

When you learned about metamorphic rocks, you found out that temperature and pressure increase as you go deeper below Earth's surface. Temperature and pressure are much greater in the mantle than in the crust. As a result, some rock in the mantle melts. This molten rock sometimes makes its way to the surface as lava.

The Inner and Outer Core

Below the mantle is Earth's core. The **core** consists of heavy material that sank to Earth's center billions of years ago. The core consists of a solid inner layer and a molten outer layer.

The outer core is made of molten iron and nickel. Scientists think the boundary between the outer core and the mantle is wavy. They think the hills and valleys in this boundary are caused by the movement of molten rock between the outer core and the mantle.

At Earth's center is the inner core, which is made of solid iron and nickel. Temperatures here may exceed 5,000°C (9,000°F)—almost as hot as the surface of the Sun! The extreme pressure here prevents the iron and nickel from melting, in spite of the high temperature.

How do you think the different layers of Earth developed? One hypothesis is that billions of years ago, energy released by the breakdown of elements inside Earth caused the planet to grow hotter and hotter. Much of the iron and nickel found in Earth's rocks melted. Because these are very heavy materials, the molten iron and nickel sank to the center of the planet. Extreme pressure turned these materials back to a solid. Lighter materials also melted, but they rose to the surface. As a result, a crust of light rock and a core of heavy metals formed, with the mantle layer in between.

Journeying to Earth's Center

You may have wondered how scientists know so much about Earth's deep layers. They certainly haven't been able to travel there! However, some rocks that have formed from magma make it possible for us to "see" the mantle. Rocks such as kimberlite that were once magma in the mantle give us clues about the composition of the mantle. But how do scientists know where the layers begin and end?

Think about the last time you tried to figure out what was inside a wrapped present. You couldn't see inside, but you could try to infer what was in the box. Scientists make inferences about Earth's layers by studying earthquake waves.

When you drop a stone in a pond, waves of energy move across the water's surface. In a similar way, when an earthquake occurs, waves of energy travel through Earth in all directions. Earthquake waves travel through some materials faster than others. By measuring the time it takes for the waves to arrive at different places around the world, scientists infer what kind of material the waves traveled through.

In 1909 the boundary between the crust and mantle was discovered by a scientist named Andrija Mohorovičic' (mō hō rō'və chich). He noticed that earthquake waves started to travel faster once they reached a certain depth below Earth's surface. Mohorovičic' inferred that there must be a different kind of rock at this depth. This boundary between the crust and the mantle, named after the man who discovered it, is called the Moho.

Two kinds of earthquake waves, called P waves and S waves, have also been used to make inferences about the properties of the core and its depth below the surface. Look at the figure on the next page to find out what scientists have learned from earthquake waves.

HOW EARTHQUAKE WAVES TRAVEL

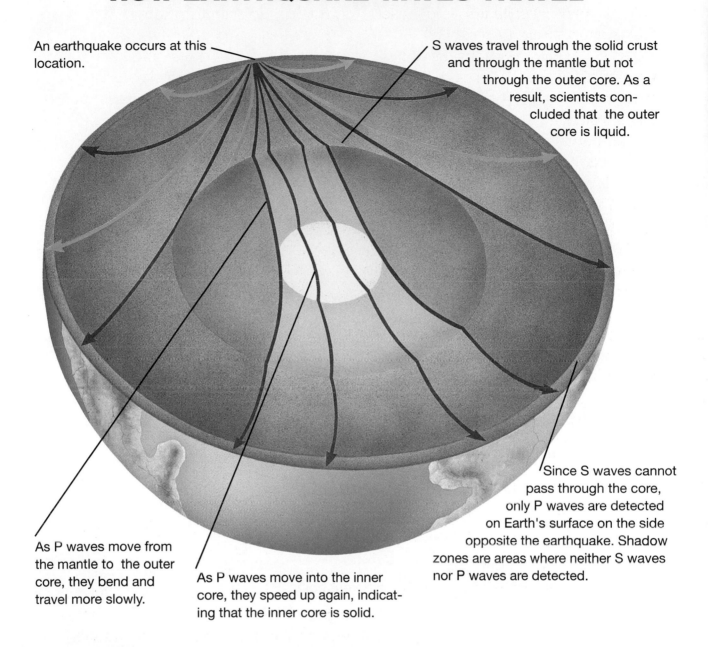

An earthquake occurs at this location.

S waves travel through the solid crust and through the mantle but not through the outer core. As a result, scientists concluded that the outer core is liquid.

As P waves move from the mantle to the outer core, they bend and travel more slowly.

As P waves move into the inner core, they speed up again, indicating that the inner core is solid.

Since S waves cannot pass through the core, only P waves are detected on Earth's surface on the side opposite the earthquake. Shadow zones are areas where neither S waves nor P waves are detected.

INVESTIGATION 1

1. Use materials of your choice to make a three-dimensional model showing Earth's layers. Make labels to identify the layers.

2. Scientists know the mass and the volume of Earth. How could this information help them make inferences about the kind of matter that makes up Earth's interior?

HOW CAN FOSSILS HELP TELL US HOW OLD A ROCK IS?

Think of Earth as a book, with layers of rock stacked on top of one another like pages. How can you use the fossils in rocks to number the pages and read the book?

Activity
Layering Fossils

Scientists study rock layers and the fossils in them to learn about ancient forms of life. Find out what scientists can learn by doing this activity.

MATERIALS

• 3 different colors of clay
• shell
• leaf
• twig
• *Science Notebook*

Procedure

1. Flatten three pieces of clay, each a different color.

2. **Make a model** of a fossil imprint by making an impression of a shell in one piece of clay. Make an impression of a leaf in the second piece of clay and a twig in the third piece of clay. Set aside the shell, leaf, and twig.

Step 2

3. Each piece of clay represents a layer of sedimentary rock. Stack your rock layers one on top of the other. In your *Science Notebook*, **record** the order from top to bottom.

Analyze and Conclude

1. Based on what you have learned about how sedimentary rock forms, **infer** which of your "fossils" would be the oldest and which would be the youngest. Explain your reasoning.

2. If the twig is from a bush that lived after the shellfish died but before the tree from which the leaf was taken lived, which fossil would be on the top of the stack? Which fossil would be on the bottom?

3. **Compare** your stack of fossils with the stacks made by other students. Are the fossils in the same order? If not, **infer** the relative ages of the fossils in each of the other stacks.

UNIT PROJECT LINK

Find out about fossils that have been collected in your community or that were discovered in your state. If possible, obtain examples of such fossils for your collection. Be sure to note the exact location where each fossil was found. If you can't get examples, make drawings of the fossils.

Activity

Finding the Order

Geologists often try to find out the order in which rock layers formed. It isn't always easy. In this activity you'll make a model of rock layers and infer the order in which they were made.

MATERIALS

- paper cups
- plastic spoons
- white glue
- food coloring, 4 colors
- sand
- wooden stick
- milk carton (1 pt)
- *Science Notebook*

Procedure

1. In a paper cup, mix a spoonful of white glue with 4 drops of red food coloring. Mix the colored glue with half a cup of sand. In the same way, make blue sand in a second cup, green sand in a third cup, and yellow sand in a fourth cup.

2. Place a small wooden stick against the inside of a milk carton. Then pack one color of sand in the bottom of the carton. Pack a second color on top of the first, and a third on top of the second.

3. Carefully pull the stick out of the carton and fill the hole with the fourth color of sand. Set the carton aside until the next day. **Predict** what the sand layers will look like when you take them out of the milk carton. In your *Science Notebook*, **draw a diagram** of your prediction.

Step 1

4. Carefully tear the milk carton away from the layers. If the glue has not dried, let it set a while longer.

5. **Compare** your layers to the drawing that you made.

6. On your drawing, number the "rock" layers from 1 to 4, with 1 representing the oldest layer, or the layer that you made first.

Analyze and Conclude

1. Which "rock" layer was laid down first? Which one "formed" last?

2. For rock layers that are horizontal, what general statement can you make about where the oldest and youngest layers are located in the stack of layers?

3. What **inference** can you make about the age of a rock layer that cuts through other layers?

INVESTIGATE FURTHER!

EXPERIMENT

Trade rock layers with another student. Infer the order in which the layers were deposited.

Sorting Through Time

People have been digging up fossils for centuries. But not until the 1700s did the idea that fossils were the remains of creatures from the past begin to be accepted. You can bet that William Smith, an English geologist, never realized that his hobby of fossil collecting would show a way of matching rock layers by age! While surveying the land in western England, Smith had a chance to observe many rock layers and collect fossils. First, he noticed that rock layers lie "like slices of bread and butter," stacked in a set order. Next, he saw that each layer of sedimentary rock contained different types of fossils. He soon realized that fossils could be used to recognize rock layers of the same age in different places around the world. And scientists today use fossils to do just that! ■

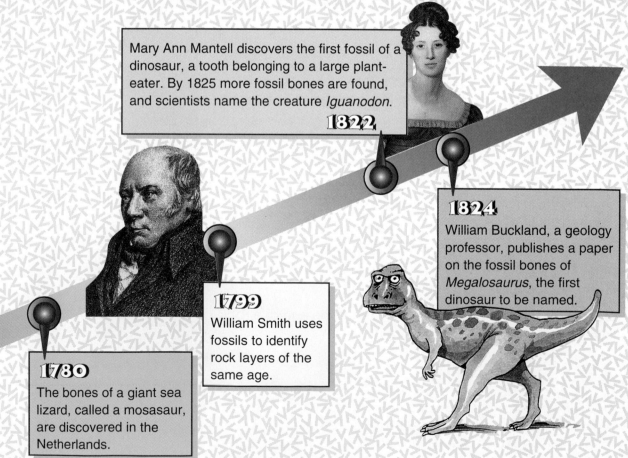

Mary Ann Mantell discovers the first fossil of a dinosaur, a tooth belonging to a large plant-eater. By 1825 more fossil bones are found, and scientists name the creature *Iguanodon*.
1822

1824
William Buckland, a geology professor, publishes a paper on the fossil bones of *Megalosaurus*, the first dinosaur to be named.

1799
William Smith uses fossils to identify rock layers of the same age.

1780
The bones of a giant sea lizard, called a mosasaur, are discovered in the Netherlands.

Fossils Tell Tales!

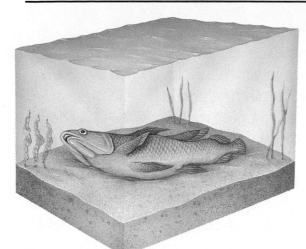

1 An organism dies.

2 The remains get buried quickly by sediment. The soft parts decay.

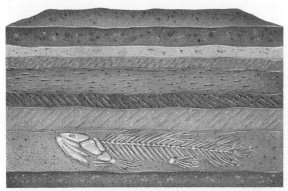

3 With time, the hard parts get replaced with minerals. The sediment layer gets buried deeper and is compacted and cemented to form sedimentary rock.

There aren't many things more exciting than coming face to face with a dinosaur—a dinosaur skeleton, that is. Our knowledge of dinosaurs has come from studying **fossils**, which are the remains and traces of living things preserved in rock. What clues do you think a fossil might provide about Earth's past? A fossil can give clues about where an organism once lived, how it may have moved, what it ate, and what it looked like, not to mention how old the rock it was found in might be.

You Old Fossil!

How does a fossil form? Many fossils form when plants and animals die and are quickly buried by clay, sand, and other sediments. Look at the drawings to see how a fossil might form.

In some cases, bone and other hard material is replaced by minerals. Other

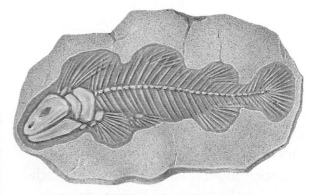

4 A fossil is later exposed due to erosion.

◀ A cast

A mold ▼

fossils form when plants and animals leave imprints in soft sediment. Over time, the organic material dissolves and the imprint gets filled with minerals or sediments. The imprint, or hollow part of the fossil, is called a mold. The material that fills in the imprint is called a cast. Remember when you pressed a shell, a leaf, and a twig into clay in the activity on pages E72 and E73? Did you make molds, or casts?

Relative Age

Scientists began studying fossils partly in the hope that fossils would help them estimate the age of Earth's rocks. There are many clues, including fossils, that you can use to learn about the ages of the rocks you see.

One clue to look for is the position of the rock layers. Recall that most sedimentary rocks begin as horizontal sediment layers. Think about books you might stack before putting them away. The first book you put down is on the bottom of the stack. It's the same with rock layers. The oldest rock layer was laid down first and is on the bottom. The youngest rock layer was laid down last and is on the top.

When you can say that one rock is older than another, you have found its relative age. A rock's **relative age** is how old it is compared to other rocks.

In addition to a rock's position, scientists also use certain kinds of fossils, called **index fossils**, to help them tell the relative ages of rock. Plant and animal species that lived for only a short time (perhaps only a few million years) but that could be found in large numbers over much of Earth make very helpful index fossils.

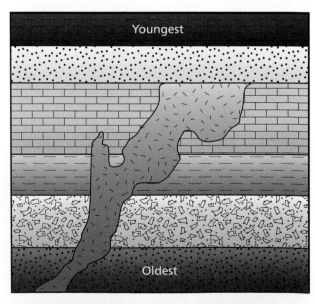

▲ **The sequence of rock layers can be used to determine the relative ages of rocks.**

The fossil shown below is a trilobite. Many kinds of trilobites lived in oceans all over the world. Since certain kinds lived only at certain times in the past, they make good index fossils. When scientists find two rocks in two different places that both contain the same kind of trilobite fossils, they know that both rocks are about the same age.

Absolute Age

When someone asks how old you are, you probably don't answer with your relative age. You probably say, "I'm 11 years old," rather than "I'm older than my sister." At times, scientists need to know more than a rock's relative age. They need to know its **absolute age**, or how old the rock really is.

Some elements found on Earth are not stable. These elements decay, or break down, into other elements at a known rate. Scientists measure how much of a decaying element is present in a rock layer and how much of the new element into which it decays is present. The amount of time required for this level of decay provides the rock's absolute age.

Potassium is an element found in rocks. Some of the potassium found in igneous and metamorphic rocks is not stable. It breaks down to form a certain kind of argon, another element. Scientists have used the amount of potassium and argon in rocks to find the absolute age of those rocks. Some were as old as a few billion years! ■

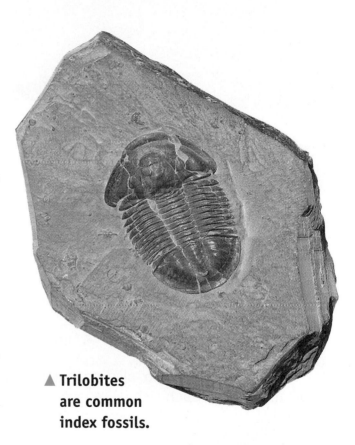

▲ Trilobites are common index fossils.

INVESTIGATION 2

1. How are index fossils used to tell the ages of rocks?

2. Suppose you and a friend each found fossils in different layers of sedimentary rock. How could you tell which fossil is older?

INVESTIGATION 3

HOW DO ROCKS BEND?

Tonight, before you climb into bed, put your hands flat on top of your covers and push them 10 or 20 cm (8 in.) across the bed. Make them push up into folds. How are these folds, or bends, like mountains?

Activity
Big Wrinkles

The Appalachian Mountains in the eastern United States are folded and eroded mountains. Geologists read them like a book. Here's how.

MATERIALS

- 3 different colors of clay
- metric ruler
- plastic knife
- *Science Notebook*

Procedure

1. Flatten three pieces of clay, each a different color, into slabs about 1 cm thick. Each slab represents a layer of rock. Stack the layers. In your *Science Notebook*, **make a sketch** to show the order of the colors from top to bottom.

2. Gently press the sides of the stack together, folding the layers upward into a mountain. Continue pressing until the sides come together.

Step 2

3. You are going to cut off the top your mountain but before you do, **predict** what the cut surface will look like. **Make a sketch** of your prediction.

4. **Model** erosion by cutting the top off your mountain with a plastic knife so you can see all three layers in the cut surface. Does it look like your prediction? **Sketch** the eroded top. Label the layers by color and title your drawing "Upward Fold."

5. Separate the three colors of clay, flatten each lump again, and make another stack. Keep the order of the colors the same as in step 1.

6. Fold the left and right sides of the stack upward until they meet, forming a mountain.

7. **Model** erosion by cutting the top off your mountain. **Make a sketch** of the eroded top. Label the layers and title your drawing "Downward Fold."

Step 6

Analyze and Conclude

1. Where was the oldest layer of rock in the stack in step 1? in the upward fold (step 4)? in the downward fold (step 7)?

2. If you know the relative ages of rock layers on an eroded surface, explain how you can tell if an upward folding of rocks or a downward folding of rocks has occurred.

UNIT PROJECT LINK

Walk around your community to observe natural landforms. Make a list of the landforms you observe. Try to identify the types of rocks that make up the different landforms. Can you tell which rock layers are oldest?

E81

Activity
Dome Questions

Some rocks get pushed up to form a geologic structure called a dome. Investigate how bending rocks can form this structure.

Procedure

1. Flatten and stack three layers of clay, each a different color. Then press the stack down over a small ball to make a dome.

Step 1

2. **Predict** what the pattern of layers will be when you cut the top off the dome. In your *Science Notebook*, **make a sketch** of your prediction.

3. **Model** erosion by cutting the top off the dome, but do not cut so deep that you can see the ball. Does the pattern of layers match your prediction? **Make a sketch** of the actual pattern and title it "Dome." Be sure to label the order of the layers.

Analyze and Conclude

1. What does the pattern of layers in a dome look like?

2. **Infer** what forces could cause a dome to form. Explain your inference.

INVESTIGATE FURTHER!

EXPERIMENT

Get an ice-cream cone of fudge-ripple ice cream. Observe the pattern of chocolate and vanilla layers. Now erode the ice cream from the top down. How does the pattern change? What kinds of "geologic structures" are you observing?

All Bent Out of Shape

No matter how hard you try, you will probably never be able to bend a rock. But mountains all over the eastern United States formed because rocks can and do bend. Let's explore how this comes about.

Forces Bend Rocks

Every time you push open a door or pull a window shut, you apply a force. A force is a push or a pull. In the activity on pages E80 and E81, you applied forces to layers of clay. You did this with your hands by pushing the clay in different directions.

Sometimes forces in nature push on rocks in the same way. If the forces are strong enough and applied long enough, they can cause the rock layers to bend. A bend in a rock layer is called a **fold**.

Most forces that bend rock layers are caused by Earth's moving plates. As you know, Earth's crust consists of huge plates that move slowly around the surface. When two plates come together, the edges of the plates may become folded. Over millions of years the folds become higher and the folded rock forms mountains.

Folded mountains form as rock layers bend and are pushed upward. ▼

The Appalachian Mountains

The Appalachian Mountains in eastern North America are mountains that formed from folded rock. This mountain range is 3,200 km (1,920 mi) long, stretching from Newfoundland in Canada to Alabama in the southeastern United States. The Appalachian Mountains formed sometime between 600 million and 200 million years ago as the plate carrying Africa collided with the plate carrying North America. With time, the folded rock formed high hills and deep valleys.

When rock layers bend, some layers fold up and some fold down. An **anticline** is an upward fold of rock layers. A **syncline** is a downward fold of rock layers.

Recall that the process of weathering wears all rocks at Earth's surface into sediments. The wearing away and removing of rock materials is called **erosion**. Gravity, moving water, wind, and ice all erode rocks. When the top of an anticline is eroded, new rock layers are revealed at the surface. Notice in the diagram on page E85 that the oldest rock layers of an anticline are found near the center of the fold. The layers get younger and younger as you move away from the center of the anticline. Now compare this to an eroded syncline. When a syncline is eroded, where is the youngest rock located? How do the anticline and syncline compare to the folded layers you created on pages E80 and E81?

SCIENCE IN LITERATURE

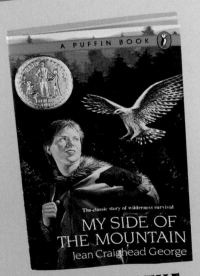

MY SIDE OF THE MOUNTAIN
by Jean Craighead George
Puffin Books, 1991

Mountains everywhere, because of their rugged terrain, are among Earth's last wild places. They are where people can go to enjoy the natural world unchanged by humans.

In *My Side of the Mountain* by Jean Craighead George, Sam Gribley escapes his crowded city apartment and finds a mountain in the Appalachian wilderness to call home. With only a ball of string, a pocket knife, and some flint and steel, he survives a whole year. Sam learns to find wild foods, build a shelter, and keep warm in blizzards. He also learns that he can rely upon himself to survive the extremes of a mountain environment.

The Appalachian Mountains are made up of many anticlines and synclines. All areas do not erode at the same rate. Some rocks are tougher than others and don't wear away easily. Rocks like sandstone and conglomerate resist erosion. Where they are exposed at the surface, these rocks form ridges. Rocks like limestone and shale wear away easily, forming valleys. The combination of folding and erosion has made the Appalachian Mountains a varied terrain. ■

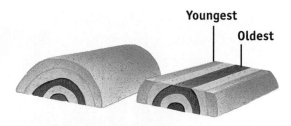

▲ **The oldest rock layers of an eroded anticline are near the center.**

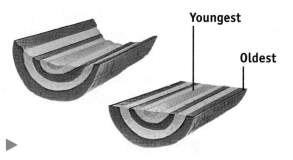

The oldest rock layers of an eroded syncline are farthest from the center. ▶

▲ **The Appalachian Mountains, which extend from the southern United States to Canada, have a varied terrain due to folding and erosion.**

The Black Hills

Forces pressing on rock from opposite sides can cause rock layers to fold. Over time, the folds may form mountains such as the Appalachians. A mountain called a dome mountain can also form from folded rock layers. The Black Hills of western South Dakota and eastern Wyoming are an example of dome mountains.

A dome mountain forms when forces deep within Earth push rock layers upward. Recall that magma can flow into existing rock. Sometimes the magma pushes the rock layers above it upward, creating a dome.

When erosion wears down the top of a dome, new rock layers are exposed. If more erosion takes place, the rock formed from magma may be exposed.

In the Black Hills, the magma that created the domes is now granite and is exposed at the surface. The center of the dome is granite surrounded by schist. How do you think the schist formed? Around the center are rings of sedimentary rock, including limestone and sandstone. The sandstone is very hard and resists erosion, forming steep ridges sometimes called hogbacks. People have also shaped the Black Hills—by carving the faces of four presidents into Mount Rushmore! ■

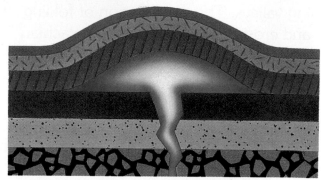

1 A dome forms when a vertical force, such as rising magma, pushes up.

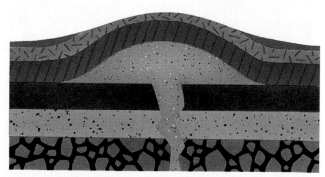

2 In a dome, the youngest rock is the igneous rock formed from the magma.

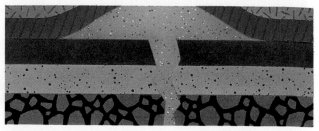

3 Erosion of a dome may expose the igneous rock formed from the magma.

Mr. President...

How many of the likenesses of former presidents carved into this mountain's granite wall can you identify? The national memorial on Mount Rushmore's northeastern side is just over 1800m high. Each head is about 30m tall.

A Real Jewel...

Jewel Cave National Monument is a 100-km long maze of underground rooms and passageways. Its caves formed long ago when water seeped underground and eroded the limestone rock layers.

INVESTIGATION 3

1. How are folded mountains different from dome mountains?

2. Imagine that you come across some folded rock layers that have been exposed by erosion. How would knowing the ages of the layers help you determine if the folding was an anticline or a syncline?

INVESTIGATION 4

WHAT IS A FAULT AND HOW CAN IT MAKE MOUNTAINS?

Mountains are big blocks of rock. You already know rock can be bent to make mountains. In this investigation you'll find out about another way that mountains are made.

Activity

It's Your Fault

Cracks and breaks in sidewalks are common. Sometimes a section of sidewalk is actually thrust up above nearby sections. Sections of rock are also thrust up to make mountains at times!

MATERIALS
- goggles
- thin wooden stick
- 2 pairs of identical books
- *Science Notebook*

SAFETY
Wear goggles.

Procedure

1. A place where rock has moved on one or both sides of a crack is called a **fault**. To **model** how a fault starts to form, have a partner hold one end of a stick down on a table, with most of the stick extending off the table.

2. Apply a gentle downward force to the free end of the stick. In your *Science Notebook*, **describe** what you **observe**. **Predict** what would happen if you applied a stronger force.

Step 2

3. Make two identical stacks of books, each consisting of two books of different sizes. The book stacks are models of rock layers.

4. Hold one stack on your right hand and the other stack on your left hand. Hold the books so that the top surfaces are level. The open sides of the books should face each other.

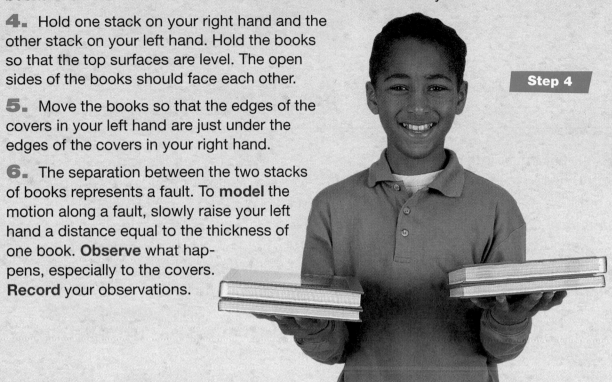

Step 4

5. Move the books so that the edges of the covers in your left hand are just under the edges of the covers in your right hand.

6. The separation between the two stacks of books represents a fault. To **model** the motion along a fault, slowly raise your left hand a distance equal to the thickness of one book. **Observe** what happens, especially to the covers. **Record** your observations.

Analyze and Conclude

1. The stick in step 2 represents rock in Earth's crust. What happens to rock if a force strong enough to bend it is applied?

2. After you raised the books in step 6, which books were beside each other on opposite sides of the fault? What do you think happens as layers of rock move vertically along a fault?

3. In step 6, did the covers of the books catch on each other? How might this be like the rocks along a fault?

INVESTIGATE FURTHER!

RESEARCH

The mountain ranges in the Great Basin of the western United States were created by faults in blocks of rock. In which states are these mountains located? What mountain ranges are part of the Great Basin?

It's So Grand

What natural wonder is 446 km (268 mi) long, up to 29 km (17 mi) wide, and more than 1.6 km (1 mi) deep? If you guessed the Grand Canyon, you're right! The Grand Canyon is cut into thousands of meters of rock! What kinds of forces could have created this amazing place? Read on to find out.

If you could peer over the edge of the canyon rim, you would see layer upon layer of rock. Long before the canyon existed, all these rock layers were formed. Recall that when rock layers are stacked one on top of the other, the oldest layer is on the bottom. The oldest rocks exposed at the very bottom of the Grand Canyon are metamorphic and igneous rocks that were formed as many as 1.5 billion years ago. The youngest rocks at the top of the rim are limestone that formed on an ocean floor 225 million years ago.

The Grand Canyon ▼

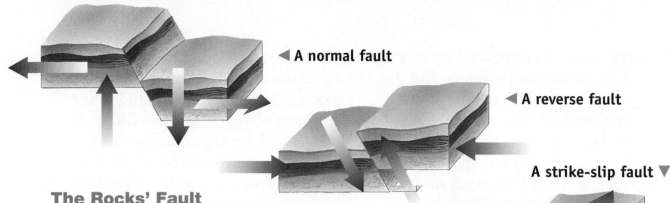

◄ **A normal fault**

◄ **A reverse fault**

A strike-slip fault ▼

The Rocks' Fault

After the rock layers in the Grand Canyon formed, a variety of events caused them to change. One such event involved forces being applied to rock, causing it to break. A break in rock along which movement has occurred is called a **fault**. As with folded rock, the forces that form faults usually are caused by Earth's moving plates.

Forces that come from different directions cause different kinds of faults to form in rock. In a game of tug of war, you pull on a rope in one direction and your friend pulls in the opposite direction. When forces on rock pull in opposite directions, a break called a normal fault can form. Notice in the diagram that rock layers on one side of the break move down in relation to those on the other side.

When moving plates caused rock in the Grand Canyon area to be stretched, many normal faults formed. Some of these faults have been given magical names, like the Crystal, Dragon, and Phantom faults. Tipoff Fault is one that cuts right across the canyon.

Recall that forces can fold rock layers into anticlines and synclines. When such pushing forces cause rock to break, a reverse fault forms. In this type of fault, rock layers on one side of the fault are pushed up in relation to those

on the other side. Use the diagram above to compare movement along a reverse fault with the movement along a normal fault.

You modeled movement along a fault in the activity on pages E88 and E89. When you moved one stack of books, books that had been next to each other weren't that way any longer. The books changed position relative to each other along the break. The same thing happens along normal and reverse faults. Older rock layers can get moved next to or even above younger rock layers. For example, just west of Las Vegas, Nevada, there is a reverse fault called the Keystone Thrust. Along this fault,

▲ **Butte Fault is one of many faults that cut through the Grand Canyon.**

limestone layers were pushed up so that they sit above sandstone layers. But the sandstone is about 300 million years younger than the limestone above it!

When blocks of rock move along normal and reverse faults, special kinds of mountains called fault-block mountains can form. Ranges of fault-block mountains occur throughout the states surrounding the Grand Canyon.

Not all movement along faults is up and down. Plate movements sometimes cause rock layers to break and slide sideways. With a strike-slip fault, rock on either side of the fault moves horizontally in opposite directions. One example of this type of fault is well known: the San Andreas Fault in California.

Carving a Canyon

Have you ever stood at the edge of the Grand Canyon? People who have are always amazed by how *big* the canyon is—photographs just can't capture its size. How do you think the canyon got carved so deep and wide?

Millions of years ago, the Colorado River flowed through northwestern Arizona just as it does today. Because it was a powerful river with a lot of fast-flowing water, it cut down into the rock over which it flowed and carried away billions of tons of sediment. Even today the Colorado River continues to erode away thousands of tons of rock material each day!

Although erosion accounts for how the Grand Canyon became so deep, the process of weathering accounts for how it became so wide. Recall that weathering is the breaking up of rock. Over time, bits of rock weathered off the sides of the canyon and fell to the bottom. There they were carried away by the river. The more rock that weathered from the canyon walls, the wider the canyon became. ∎

The power of the Colorado River carved the Grand Canyon and today propels these white-water rafters. ▼

Earthquake!

▲ **Bridge damaged by the 1994 Los Angeles earthquake**

Can you imagine how scary it must be to wake up with the room shaking around you? That's what happened to millions of people around Los Angeles in 1994. The ground was shaking because an earthquake had begun along a fault in California.

Why did this happen? As you have learned, forces within Earth can cause rock to break and move. When this occurs, energy is released. As a result, the ground shakes. This shaking of the ground is called an earthquake. Movement along a fault is not the only thing that causes an earthquake, although it is the most common cause.

The place where movement first occurs along a fault is below Earth's surface and is called the focus. The place on Earth's surface above the focus is called the epicenter.

Have you ever struck a bell to make it ring? If so, you know it starts to vibrate. In the same way, waves of energy move out from the focus and start the ground shaking. These waves damage land and buildings. In general, as the depth of the focus increases, so does the size of the area that will be damaged by the earthquake waves.

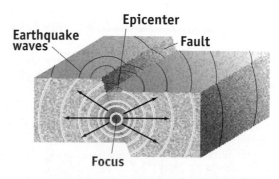

▲ **Earthquakes occur when there is movement along a fault.**

Why do you think earthquakes don't occur all the time along the system of faults under California? Faults are jagged and rough. So as plates move, sections of rock on either side catch on each other and lock together. Eventually enough force builds up so that the rocks unlock and slip past each other. This sudden movement causes an earthquake.

Most earthquakes occur at shallow depths, above 650 km (400 mi). Below this depth, temperature and pressure are so high that all rock bends and flows rather than breaks. Along the famous San Andreas Fault, most earthquakes occur at depths less than 30 km (18 mi).

There have been major earthquakes along the San Andreas Fault. In 1857, a section of the fault 120 km (74 mi) from Los Angeles moved 9 m (30 ft). In 1906 the fault shifted 6 m (20 ft) and the earthquake that resulted destroyed San Francisco. Since scientists believe the San Andreas Fault is about 20 million years old, you can bet there were many more major earthquakes along this fault before such occurrences were recorded.

Slow movement occurs along the San Andreas Fault all the time. Each year, crust along the fault moves several centimeters. Scientists believe that in about 10 million years, Los Angeles will have moved so far north that it will sit just across the fault from San Francisco! In about 60 million years, it will be completely separated from the rest of California. As long as the crust along the San Andreas Fault continues to move, earthquakes will keep happening, and the residents of California must keep expecting them. ■

▲ **Signs of movement along the San Andreas Fault**

INVESTIGATION 4

1. How do faults result in the formation of mountains?

2. Along what type of fault is a mountain not likely to occur? Explain your answer.

WORD POWER

fault	fossil
anticline	index fossil
core	mantle
crust	model
erosion	relative age
fold	syncline
absolute age	

On Your Own
Review the terms in the list. Then use as many terms as you can in a paragraph about Earth's structure.

With a Partner
Write a definition for each term in the list. Have your partner match each definition to the correct term.

PORTFOLIO
Collect pictures from magazines that show rock formations of various kinds. Try to identify faults, folds, and other features in the pictures.

Analyze Information
Study the drawing. Then identify the layers of Earth shown.

Assess Performance
Using materials of your choice, model movement along the three types of faults. Describe the forces acting in each case.

Problem Solving

1. Compare and contrast folding and faulting.

2. A sandstone layer is found atop a shale layer. A thick section of gabbro, which hardened from magma, cuts upward through both layers. A fault cuts through all three rocks. What are the relative ages of the fault and the three rock layers? Explain your reasoning.

3. Make a sketch of a syncline and an anticline. Then make a sketch showing the eroded top of each formation. Label the rock layers from oldest to youngest in each sketch.

Throughout this unit, you've investigated questions related to Earth and its structures. How will you use what you've learned and share that information with others? Here are some ideas.

Hold a Big Event
to Share Your Unit Project

Set up a rock, mineral, and fossil exhibit using the collections your group and the other groups assembled. Prepare identification cards for each sample. Also publish a guide to rocks, minerals, and fossils for your area. Distribute copies to parents and friends who attend the exhibit and invite them to use the guide to learn about the types of rocks, minerals, and fossils present in your community.

Experiment

With the help of a mineral guide and a hand lens, classify your minerals based on crystal structure. You might also grow crystal gardens, using different materials—alum, salt, sugar, and so on. Try adding a few drops of food coloring to each solution. What happens to the crystals? When the crystals are grown, examine them with a microscope or hand lens. Which crystals look like the cubes? Which have six faces? What other shapes of crystals did you grow? Draw and label the characterstcs of the crystals in your *Science Notebook*.

Research

Which topic in this unit would you like to investigate further? Try finding out more about rock layers or erosion. (You might wish to ask a partner to work with you.) To do so, locate a rock face or any rock formation where you can observe layers of rocks. Study the rock formation as closely as you can. Sketch or photograph the layers. Take rock samples. If possible, ask a geologist to help you interpret what you see. Then assemble your research into an informative display.

SCIENCE Handbook

THINK LIKE A SCIENTIST

You don't have to be a professional scientist to act and think like one. Thinking like a scientist mostly means using common sense. It also means learning how to test your ideas in a careful way.

In other words, *you* can think like a scientist.

Make a Hypothesis

Plan and Do a Test

Make Observations

To think like a scientist, you should learn as much as you can by observing things around you. Everything you hear and see is a clue about how the natural world works.

Ask a Question

Look for patterns. You'll get ideas and ask questions like these:

- Do all birds eat the same seeds?
- How does the time that the Sun sets change from day to day?

Make a Guess Called a Hypothesis

If you have an idea about why or how something happens, make an educated guess, or *hypothesis*, that you can test. For example, let's suppose that your hypothesis about the sunset time is that it changes by one minute each day.

Plan and Do a Test

Plan how to test your hypothesis. Your plan would need to consider some of these problems:

- How will you measure the time that the Sun sets?
- Will you measure the time every day?
- For how many days or weeks do you need to measure?

Record and Analyze What Happens

When you test your idea, you need to observe carefully and write down, or record, everything that happens. When you finish collecting data, you may need to do some calculations with it. For example, you might want to calculate how much the sunset time changes in a week or a month.

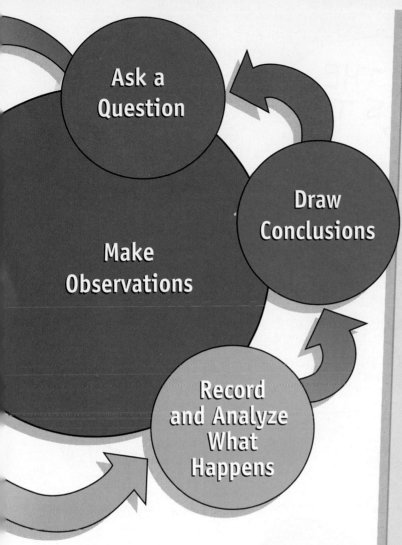

Ask a
Question

Draw
Conclusions

Make
Observations

Record
and Analyze
What
Happens

Draw Conclusions

Whatever happens in a test, think about all the reasons for your results. For example, you might wonder what causes the time of sunset to change. You might also ask when the earliest and latest sunsets occur during the year. Sometimes this thinking leads to a new hypothesis.

If the time of the sunset changes by one minute each day, think about what else the data shows you. Can you predict the time that the Sun will set one month from now?

To think like a scientist, you need to practice certain ways of thinking.

Always check for yourself.
Always ask, "How do I really know it's true?" Be willing to find out for yourself.

Be honest and careful about what you observe.
It's easy to only look for the results you expect. It's harder to see the unexpected. But unexpected results lead scientists to ask more questions. They also provide information on how things work.

Don't be afraid to be wrong.
Based on their observations, scientists make many hypotheses. Not all of these hypotheses turn out to be correct. But scientists can learn from wrong "guesses," because even wrong guesses result in information that leads to knowledge.

Keep an open mind about possible explanations.
Make sure to think about all the reasons why something might have happened. Consider all the explanations that you can think of.

WHAT CAUSES THE ROCK IN STATUES TO WEAR AWAY?

Make Observations

Ask a Question

Donelle and Ramon were walking through downtown when Ramon pointed to a statue, laughed, and said, "Look, that poor guy's nose has fallen off." Donelle laughed and as they both took a closer look at the statue, they could see that most of the statue's face was missing. Even the statue's body was pitted.

Donelle thought she knew why. She suspected that rain, snow, and ice were destroying the statue. "But it's stone," Ramon argued. "Stone doesn't dissolve in water. Does it?" "But don't we get acid rain here?" Donelle replied. "Maybe acid rain destroys stone."

The next day in school, Donelle described the "melting" statue to the class. Mr. Reynolds, their teacher, suggested that the class set up an experiment to find out what might be causing the damage to the statue. To begin, they came up with some questions that they wanted to answer.

What is destroying this statue?

Is rain destroying this statue?

Are cold winter temperatures destroying this statue?

The class decided that the first question was not specific enough. They

Here's an example of an everyday problem and how thinking like a scientist can help you explore it.

Make Observations

Make a Hypothesis

Before the class could begin setting up an experiment, there were some things they had to find out about the problem. First, they had to find out what the statue was made of. Ramon contacted City Hall and found out that the statue was made out of a stone called limestone.

Donelle told her classmates that she thought that the rain that fell on their town was sometimes acid. So Donelle and her classmates took samples of rainwater. They tested the rainwater with litmus paper and discovered that the rain was acidic.

The class thought about the new information they now had. It was time to use this information to formulate a hypothesis that they could test. Their hypothesis was "Acid rain eats away limestone."

decided to test whether rain could be destroying the statue. Students were curious about whether pollution in the air, and thus in the rain, might be affecting the statue.

Scientific investigations usually begin with something that you have noticed or read about. As you think about what you already know, you'll discover some ideas that you're not sure about. This will help you to ask the question that you really want to answer.

When you use what you have observed to suggest a possible answer to your question, you are making a *hypothesis*. Be sure that your hypothesis is an idea that you can test somehow. If you can't think of an experiment or a model to test your hypothesis, try changing it. Sometimes it's better to make a simpler, clearer hypothesis that answers only part of your question.

Plan and Do a Test

Make Observations

Ramon, Donelle, and their classmates designed a way to test their hypothesis. First, Mr. Reynolds got some fairly equal-sized lumps of limestone for the class to use. Donelle set up three flat-bottomed beakers big enough to hold the chunks of limestone. Ramon created a table for recording information.

The students had discussed what kind of solutions they should use in each beaker. They decided to put rain-water they'd collected in one beaker. They decided to put a more acidic solution in the second beaker. Mr. Reynolds provided them with a solution of weak sulfuric acid. The students knew that the third beaker should contain only pure, distilled water.

The third beaker served as the students' control. The control part of an experiment is almost identical to the other parts of the experiment. It is different in just one way: it doesn't have the condition that is being tested. In this case, the class was testing the effects on lime-stone of water that is acidic. To make sure that their results only reflect the effects of acid, and not something else that might be in water, the students set up a control in which acid was missing.

After the three beakers were each filled with their specific liquid and labeled, the students found the mass of each chunk of limestone and then put one in each beaker.

The students placed the beakers on a lab table at the back of the classroom. A square piece of glass was placed over each beaker to keep out dirt and dust that might affect the results.

One way to try out your hypothesis is to use a test called an experiment. When you plan an experiment, be sure that it helps you to answer your question. But even when you plan, things can happen that make the experiment confusing or make it not work properly. If this happens, you can change the plan or the experiment, and try again.

Record and Analyze What Happened

Make Observations

After seven days, the mass of each limestone chunk was found again. The mass was recorded on the chart on the board. The chunk was replaced in the same beaker. This was repeated every seven days.

The students recorded the mass of the limestone chunks for fourteen weeks. At the end of the experiment, their chart looked like the one on the next page.

The students analyzed the data on their chart. Donelle noted that the more acidic the solution in the beaker, the more mass the limestone "lost." Ramon noted that the mass of the limestone in the beaker containing distilled water remained the same. The limestone in the rainwater beaker "lost" some mass, but not as much as the limestone chunk in the beaker containing sulfuric acid.

Mass of Limestone Each Week (in grams)

	Week													
	1	2	3	4	5	6	7	8	9	10	11	12	13	14
Rainwater	83	83	82	82	81	80	80	79	79	78	77	77	76	75
Sulfuric acid solution	76	74	71	69	68	65	63	60	59	55	53	50	48	45
Distilled water	79	79	79	79	79	79	79	79	79	79	79	79	79	79

When you do an experiment, you need to write down, or record, your observations. Some of your observations might be numbers of things that you counted or measured. Your recorded observations are called data. When you record your data, you need to organize it in a way that helps you to understand it. Graphs and tables are helpful ways to organize data. Then think about the information you have collected. Analyze what it tells you.

Make Observations

Draw Conclusions

Both Ramon and Donelle thought that it looked like their hypothesis was supported. Water containing an acid, or acid rain, did eat away limestone. But Ramon was still not completely satisfied. He wondered if acid rain affected all kinds of stone in the same way, or if it destroyed only limestone. Ramon posed his question to Mr. Reynolds and the other students. Then Patrick added, "And I wonder if cold weather makes the effects of acid rain even worse."

It was soon evident that though their experiment had showed that acid rain does affect limestone, a whole new set of questions occurred to them.

After you have analyzed your data, you should use what you have learned to draw a conclusion. A conclusion is a statement that sums up what you learned. The conclusion should be about the question you asked. Think about whether the information you have gathered supports your hypothesis or not. If it does, figure out how to test out your idea more thoroughly. Also think about new questions you can ask.

SAFETY

The best way to be safe in the classroom is to use common sense. Prepare yourself for each activity before you start it. Get help from your teacher when there is a problem. Most important of all, pay attention. Here are some other ways that you can stay safe.

Stay Safe From Stains

- Wear protective clothing or an old shirt when you work with messy materials.
- If anything spills, wipe it up or ask your teacher to help you clean it up.

Stay Safe From Flames

- Keep your clothes away from open flames. If you have long or baggy sleeves, roll them up.
- Don't let your hair get close to a flame. If you have long hair, tie it back.

Stay Safe From Injuries

- Protect your eyes by wearing safety goggles when you are told that you need them.
- Keep your hands dry around electricity. Water is a good conductor of electricity, so you can get a shock more easily if your hands are wet.
- Be careful with sharp objects. If you have to press on them, keep the sharp side away from you.
- Cover any cuts you have that are exposed. If you spill something on a cut, be sure to wash it off immediately.
- Don't eat or drink anything unless your teacher tells you that it's okay.

Stay Safe During Cleanup

- Wash up after you finish working.
- Dispose of things in the way that your teachers tells you to.

MOST IMPORTANTLY

If you ever hurt yourself or one of your group members gets hurt, tell your teacher right away.

DON'T MAKE A MESS If you spill something, clean it up right away. When finished with an activity, clean up your work area. Dispose of things in the way your teacher tells you to.

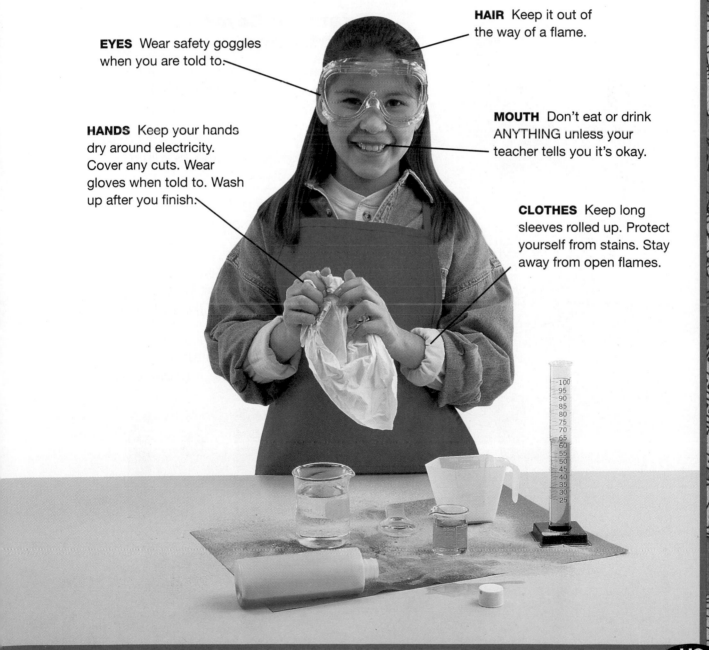

HAIR Keep it out of the way of a flame.

EYES Wear safety goggles when you are told to.

MOUTH Don't eat or drink ANYTHING unless your teacher tells you it's okay.

HANDS Keep your hands dry around electricity. Cover any cuts. Wear gloves when told to. Wash up after you finish.

CLOTHES Keep long sleeves rolled up. Protect yourself from stains. Stay away from open flames.

Using a Microscope

A microscope makes it possible to see very small things by magnifying them. Some microscopes have a set of lenses to magnify objects different amounts.

Examine Some Salt Grains

Handle a microscope carefully; it can break easily. Carry it firmly with both hands and avoid touching the lenses.

1. Turn the mirror toward a source of light. **NEVER** use the Sun as a light source.

2. Place a few grains of salt on the slide. Put the slide on the stage of the microscope.

3. While looking through the eyepiece, turn the adjustment knob on the back of the microscope to bring the salt grains into focus.

4. Raise the eyepiece tube to increase the magnification; lower it to decrease magnification.

Using a
Calculator

After you've made measurements, a calculator can help you analyze your data. Some calculators have a memory key that allows you to save the result of one calculation while you do another.

Find an Average

The table shows the amount of rain that was collected using a rain gauge in each month of one year. You can use a calculator to help you find the average monthly rainfall.

1. Add the numbers. When you add a series of numbers, you don't need to press the equal sign until the last number is entered. Just press the plus sign after you enter each number (except the last one).

2. If you make a mistake while you are entering numbers, try to erase your mistake by pushing the clear entry (CE) key or the clear (C) key. Then you can continue entering the rest of the numbers you are adding. If you can't fix your mistake, you can push the (C) key once or twice until the screen shows 0. Then start over.

3. Your total should be 1,131. You can use the total to find the average. Just divide by the number of months in the year.

Rainfall	
Month	**Rain (mm)**
Jan.	214
Feb.	138
Mar.	98
Apr.	157
May	84
June	41
July	5
Aug.	23
Sept.	48
Oct.	75
Nov.	140
Dec.	108

These keys run the calculator's memory functions.

This key erases the last entry.

Using a Balance

A balance is used to measure mass. Mass is the amount of matter in an object. Place the object to be massed in the left pan. Place standard masses in the right pan.

Measure the Mass of an Orange

1. Check that the empty pans are balanced, or level with each other. The pointer at the base should be on the middle mark. If it needs to be adjusted, move the slider on the back of the balance a little to the left or right.

2. Place an orange on the left pan. Notice that the pointer moves and that the pans are no longer level with each other. Then add standard masses, one at a time, to the right pan. When the pointer is at the middle mark again, the pans are balanced. Each pan holds the same amount of mass.

3. Each standard mass is marked to show the number of grams it contains. Add the number of grams marked on the masses in the pan. The total is the mass in grams of the orange.

Using a Spring Scale

A spring scale is used to measure force.
You can use a spring scale to find the weight
of an object in newtons. You can also use
the scale to measure other forces.

Measure the Weight of an Object

1. Place the object in a net bag, and hang it from the hook on the bottom of the spring scale. Or, if possible, hang the object directly from the hook.

2. Slowly lift the scale by the top hook. Be sure the object to be weighed continues to hang from the bottom hook.

3. Wait until the pointer on the face of the spring scale has stopped moving. Read the number next to the pointer to determine the weight of the object in newtons.

Measure Friction

1. Hook the object to the bottom of the spring scale. Use a rubber band to connect the spring scale and object if needed.

2. Gently pull the top hook of the scale parallel to the floor. When the object starts to move, read the number of newtons next to the pointer on the scale. This number is the force of friction between the floor and the object as you drag the object.

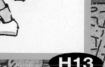

Using a Thermometer

A thermometer is used to measure temperature. When the liquid in the tube of a thermometer gets warmer, it expands and moves farther up the tube. Different units can be used to measure temperature, but scientists usually use the Celsius scale.

Measure the Temperature of a Cold Liquid

1. Half-fill a cup with chilled liquid.

2. Hold the thermometer so that the bulb is in the center of the liquid.

3. Wait until you see the liquid in the tube stop moving. Read the scale line that is closest to the top of the liquid in the tube.

Measuring Volume

A graduated cylinder, a measuring cup, and a beaker are used to measure volume. Volume is the amount of space something takes up. Most of the containers that scientists use to measure volume have a scale marked in milliliters (mL).

Measure the Volume of Juice

1. Pour the juice into a measuring container.

2. Move your head so that your eyes are level with the top of the juice. Read the scale line that is closest to the surface of the juice. If the surface of the juice is curved up on the sides, look at the lowest point of the curve.

3. You can estimate the value between two lines on the scale to obtain a more accurate measurement.

▲ The bottom of the curve is at 50 mL.

This beaker has marks for each 25 mL. ▼

This graduated cylinder has marks for every 1 mL. ▶

This measuring cup has marks for each 25 mL. ▼

Each container above has 50 mL of juice.

MEASUR

Area
A basketball court covers about 4,700 ft². It covers about 435 m².

Volume
1 L of sports drink is a little more than 1 qt.

Temperature
The temperature at an indoor basketball game might be 25°C, which is 77°F.

SI Measures

Temperature
Ice melts at 0 degrees Celsius (°C)

Water freezes at 0°C

Water boils at 100°C

Length and Distance
1,000 meters (m) = 1 kilometer (km)

100 centimeters (cm) = 1 m

10 millimeters (mm) = 1 cm

Force
1 newton (N) =
1 kilogram x meter/second/second
(kg x m/s²)

Volume
1 cubic meter (m³) = 1 m x 1 m x 1 m

1 cubic centimeter (cm³) =
1 cm x 1 cm x 1 cm

1 liter (L) = 1,000 milliliters (mL)

1 cm³ = 1 mL

Area
1 square kilometer (km²) = 1 km x 1 km

1 hectare = 10,000 m²

Mass
1,000 grams (g) = 1 kilogram (kg)

1,000 milligrams (mg) = 1 g

EMENTS

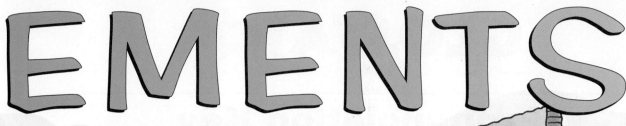

Mass and Weight
A basketball has a mass of about 650 g.
It weighs about $1\frac{1}{2}$-lb.

Length/ Distance
A basketball rim is about
10 ft high, or a little more
than 3 m from the floor.

Rates (SI and English)
km/h = kilometers per hour

m/s = meters per second

mph = miles per hour

English Measures

Volume of Fluids
8 fluid ounces (fl oz) = 1 cup (c)

2 c = 1 pint (pt)

2 pt = 1 quart (qt)

4 qt = 1 gallon (gal)

Temperature
Ice melts at 32 degrees
Fahrenheit (°F)

Water freezes at 32°F

Water boils at 212°F

Length and Distance
12 inches (in.) = 1 foot (ft)

3 ft = 1 yard (yd)

5,280 ft = 1 mile (mi)

Weight
16 ounces (oz) = 1 pound (lb)   2,000 pounds = 1 ton (T)

GLOSSARY

Pronunciation Key

Symbol	Key Words	Symbol	Key Words
a	cat	g	get
ā	ape	h	help
ä	cot, car	j	jump
		k	kiss, call
e	ten, berry	l	leg
ē	me	m	meat
		n	nose
i	fit, here	p	put
ī	ice, fire	r	red
		s	see
ō	go	t	top
ô	fall, for	v	vat
oi	oil	w	wish
oo	look, pull	y	yard
ōō	tool, rule	z	zebra
ou	out, crowd		
		ch	chin, arch
u	up	ŋ	ring, drink
ʉ	fur, shirt	sh	she, push
		th	thin, truth
ə	**a** in ago	_th_	then, father
	e in agent	zh	measure
	i in pencil		
	o in atom	
	u in circus	
b	bed	
d	dog	
f	fall	

A heavy stress mark ′ is placed after a syllable that gets a heavy, or primary, stress, as in **picture** (pik′chər).

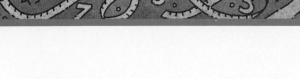

absolute age The actual age of an object. (E79) The *absolute age* of this statue is 3,500 years.

absolute magnitude The measure of a star's brightness, based on the amount of light it actually gives off. (B61) The Sun's *absolute magnitude* is less than that of many stars, but its apparent magnitude exceeds that of any other star.

adaptation (ad əp tā'shən) A structure or behavior that enables an organism to survive in its environment. (A70, A86) The thick fur of some animals is an *adaptation* to cold environments.

addiction (ə dik'shən) A condition in which a person has extreme difficulty in stopping the use of a drug. (G51) Sometimes it takes only a short time to develop an *addiction* to a drug.

alcohol (al'kə hôl) A drug that is found in some beverages, such as beer and wine. (G50) If a person drinks *alcohol* to excess, problems can occur.

alcoholism (al'kə hôl iz əm) A disease that results from the continual misuse of alcohol. (G60) Doctors continue to learn more about *alcoholism*.

amplitude (am'plə tōōd) A measure of the amount of energy in a sound wave. (F57) The *amplitude* of a loud sound is greater than the amplitude of a soft sound.

anticline (an'ti klīn) An upward fold of rock layers. (E84) Bending layers of rock formed an *anticline*.

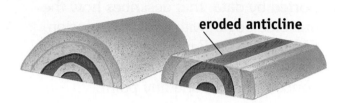

eroded anticline

apparent magnitude The measure of a star's brightness as seen from Earth. (B61) A star's *apparent magnitude* depends on the amount of light it gives off and on its distance from Earth.

asexual reproduction (ā sek'shōō əl rē prə duk'shən) A process in which offspring are produced from one or more cells of a single parent. (A62) In *asexual reproduction*, the offspring is identical to the parent.

audiocassette (ô'dē ō kə set) A small container holding magnetic tape that is used for playing or recording sound. (F92) We inserted an *audiocassette* into the tape recorder.

auditory nerve (ô'də tôr ē nʉrv) A nerve in the ear that carries nerve impulses to the brain. (G39, F85) The *auditory nerve* contains sensory neurons.

axis The imaginary line on which an object rotates. (B13) Earth's *axis* runs between the North and South poles.

B

Big Bang Theory A hypothesis, supported by data, that describes how the universe began with a huge explosion. (B39) The *Big Bang Theory* holds that everything in the universe was once concentrated at one tiny point.

biodiversity (bī ō də vʉr′sə tē) The variety of organisms that live in Earth's many ecosystems; the variety of plants and animals that live within a particular ecosystem. (D58) The *biodiversity* of an ecosystem quickly changes after a natural disaster.

biome (bī′ōm) A major land ecosystem having a distinct combination of plants and animals. (D48) Some *biomes*, such as the tundra, do not easily support human populations.

biosphere (bī′ō sfir) A self-sustaining natural system of living things and their environment. (B87) For humans to survive in space, they must bring along a version of their *biosphere*.

black dwarf The cool, dark body that is the final stage in the life cycle of a low-mass star. (B66) When the Sun dies, it will become a *black dwarf*.

black hole An extremely dense, invisible object in space whose gravity is so great that not even light can escape it. (B67) Scientists think that the remains of a very massive star can collapse following a supernova explosion to form a *black hole*.

blood alcohol concentration A test that determines the level of alcohol in a person's blood. (G61) A police officer can easily find out if a driver is drunk by giving a *blood alcohol concentration* test.

bone The hard tissue that forms the skeleton. Also, one of the organs that makes up the skeleton. (G8) The human hand contains many small *bones*.

C

caffeine (ka fēn′) A drug that acts as a stimulant and is present in coffee, many teas, cocoa, and some soft drinks. (G50) Many people prefer to drink herbal teas that do not have *caffeine* in them.

carbon dioxide–oxygen cycle *See* oxygen–carbon dioxide cycle.

cardiac muscle (kär′dē ak mus′əl) Involuntary muscle tissue that makes up the heart. (G17) *Cardiac muscle* contracts rhythmically.

carnivore (kär′nə vôr) A consumer that eats only other animals. (D19, D30) Lions are *carnivores* that prey on zebras and other large plant eaters.

cartilage (kärt′ə·l ij) Tough, flexible tissue that is part of the skeleton. (G8) *Cartilage* helps protect bones as they move at joints.

cell The basic unit of structure of all living things. (A24) Even though plant *cells* can be different sizes, they still have many of the same structures.

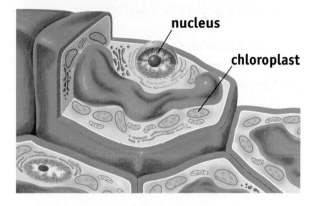

nucleus

chloroplast

cell membrane A thin layer that surrounds all cells and allows water and dissolved materials to pass into and out of the cell. (A24) In plant cells, the *cell membrane* lies inside the cell wall.

cell respiration The process of using oxygen to release energy from food. (A35, A45, D34) Animals and plants release carbon dioxide as a waste product of *cell respiration.*

cell wall The tough outer covering of a plant cell that gives the cell its rigid shape. (A24) A *cell wall* is not found in animal cells.

cementation (sē men tā′shən) A process in which minerals, deposited as water evaporates, bind sediments into solid rock. (E44) Sandstone is a sedimentary rock formed by *cementation.*

cerebellum (ser ə bel′əm) The second largest part of the brain, coordinating the body's muscles. (G32) The *cerebellum* allows smooth movement.

cerebrum (sə rē′brəm) The largest part of the brain in which the processes of thinking, learning, and reasoning take place. (G31) The *cerebrum* is the part of the brain that allows people to understand and remember ideas.

chloroplast (klôr′ə plast) A structure in plant cells that captures light energy that is used in the food-making process. (A33) *Chloroplasts* are located within cells in the leaves of a plant.

cleavage (klēv′ij) The tendency of some minerals to split along flat surfaces. (E15) Salt, or halite, shows *cleavage* in three planes.

clone (klōn) An exact copy of a parent organism produced by asexual reproduction. (A62) One way to *clone* a parent plant is to place a cutting from that plant in water.

coastal ocean A saltwater ecosystem that is relatively shallow and close to the shoreline and that supports an abundance of life. (D54) The *coastal ocean* is an ecosystem that lies beyond the shoreline.

comet (käm′it) A small object in space, made of ice, dust, gas, and rock, that orbits a star and that can form a gaseous tail. (B24) As a *comet* approaches the Sun, it begins to melt.

commensalism (kə men'səl iz əm) A close relationship between two kinds of organisms that benefits one of the organisms while neither benefiting nor hurting the other. (D21) The way that some insects use their resemblance to plants to hide from predators is an example of *commensalism*.

community (kə myoō'nə tē) All the organisms living together in a particular ecosystem. (D10) Raccoons, deer, and trees are part of a forest *community*.

compact disc (käm'pakt disk) A small disk on which sounds are digitally recorded and played back when read by a laser beam. (F92) This *compact disc*, or CD, contains one hour of music.

compound machine A machine that is made up of two or more simple machines. (C62) A pair of scissors is a *compound machine* because it contains two kinds of simple machines—a lever and a wedge.

compound microscope A viewing instrument that uses two lenses to magnify objects many times. (F41) The human hair appeared 1,000 times larger than actual size under the *compound microscope*.

compression (kəm presh'ən) A region in a sound wave where particles have been pushed together. (F57) The *compressions* produced by a vibrating tuning fork are areas of greater than normal air pressure.

concave lens (kän'kāv lenz) A lens that is thicker at the edges than it is in the middle and that causes light rays to spread apart. (F32) A *concave lens* is used to correct nearsightedness.

concave mirror A mirror that curves inward at the middle. (F23) A *concave mirror* is used in a reflecting telescope.

concrete (kän'krēt) A mixture of rock material and cement that is used as a building material. (E24) This sidewalk is made of *concrete*.

condensation (kän dən sā'shən) The process by which water vapor is changed to liquid water. (D36) *Condensation* can occur on a glass containing ice cubes.

conduction (kən duk'shən) The transfer of heat energy by direct contact between particles. (C13) Heat travels through a metal by *conduction*.

conifer (kän'ə fər) A tree or shrub that bears its seeds in cones. (A80) The cones of each species of *conifer* are distinct and different from each other.

constellation (kän stə lā'shən) A group of stars that form a fixed pattern in the night sky. (B10) The *constellation* Orion is best seen in the winter.

consumer (kən soōm'ər) A living thing that obtains energy by eating other living things. (A36, D19) Meat eaters and plant eaters are *consumers*.

contact lens A thin lens worn over the cornea of the eye, usually to correct vision problems. (F35) Some people use *contact lenses* rather than eyeglasses to improve their vision.

convection (kən vek'shən) The transfer of heat energy through liquids and gases by moving particles. (C13) Heat is carried throughout water in a pot on the stove by *convection*.

convex lens (kän'veks lenz) A lens that is thicker in the middle than at the edges and that brings light rays together. (F32) A *convex lens* is used to correct farsightedness.

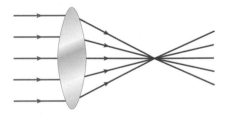

convex mirror A mirror that curves outward at the middle. (F23) The side-view mirror of a car is a *convex mirror*.

core The innermost layer of Earth, which consists of a molten outer part and a solid inner part. (E69) Temperatures inside the *core* of Earth are nearly as hot as those on the Sun's surface.

crest The highest point of a wave. (F57) The top of a water wave is its *crest*.

crust The outer layer of Earth. (E68) Earth's *crust* is a thin layer of rock.

cytoplasm (sīt'ō plaz əm) The jellylike substance that fills much of the cell. (A24) The nucleus, vacuoles, and many other cell structures float in the *cytoplasm*.

decibel (des'ə bəl) A unit used to measure the loudness or intensity of sound. (F79) Sounds that have an intensity greater than 120 *decibels* (db) can hurt your ears.

decomposer (dē kəm pōz'ər) A living thing that breaks down the remains of dead organisms. (A37, D19) *Decomposers*, such as bacteria, get their energy from the dead plants and animals they break down.

deciduous forest (dē sij'o͞o əs fôr'ist) A biome that contains many trees and in which rainfall is moderate. (D51) *Deciduous forests* support a great variety of animal life.

deforestation (dē fôr is tā'shən) A mass clearing of a forest. (A93) *Deforestation* is a major concern of environmentalists.

desert A biome in which plant life is not abundant and rainfall is low. (D50) Because *deserts* are dry, desert plants have adaptations to conserve water.

dicot (dī'kät) A flowering plant that produces seeds with two seed leaves, or food-storing leaves. (A81) A trait of a *dicot* is that its leaves have netlike veins.

drug A substance, other than food, that can affect the function of body cells and tissues and that produces a change in the body. (G50) A person sometimes takes a pain-killing *drug* after suffering a back injury.

ecosystem (ek'ō sis təm) An area in which living and nonliving things interact. (D10) An oak tree and the organisms that inhabit it can be thought of as a small *ecosystem*.

effort force The force that must be applied to an object to move the object. (C30) The tow truck applied enough *effort force* to pull the car away.

electromagnetic radiation (ē lek trō mag net'ik rā dē ā'shən) Wave energy given off by the Sun and some other objects. (F8) Visible light is a form of *electromagnetic radiation*.

electron microscope (ē lek'trän mī'krə skōp) A viewing instrument that magnifies objects thousands of times by using a beam of electrons instead of a beam of light. (F43) Doctors studied the virus through an *electron microscope*.

embryo (em'brē ō) An organism in its earliest stages of development; in most plants it is found inside a seed. (A61) When conditions for growth are suitable, the *embryo* inside the seed develops into a young plant.

endangered In danger of becoming extinct. (A92, D61) As the destruction of the Amazon rain forest continues, the number of *endangered* species increases.

energy The ability to do work or cause change. (C9, F8) *Energy* from the Sun warms the air.

erosion (ē rō'zhən) The wearing away and removing of rock and soil caused by such forces as wind and flowing water. (E84) The pounding waves caused *erosion* of the sandy shoreline.

Eustachian tube (yo͞o stā'kē ən to͞ob) A tube that connects the throat and the middle ear. (F85) The *Eustachian tube* equalizes the air pressure on both sides of the eardrum.

evaporation (ē vap ə rā'shən) The process by which liquid water changes to water vapor. (D36) One phase of the water cycle is the *evaporation* of water from lakes, rivers, and oceans.

extinct (ek stiŋkt') No longer living as a species. (A92, D61) Traces of some *extinct* species can be found in fossils.

extraterrestrial (eks trə tə res'trē əl) A being from outer space; any object from beyond Earth. (B90) It would be extraordinary for scientists to discover that there is *extraterrestrial* life.

fault A break in rock along which rocks have moved. (E91) Forces within Earth's crust produce *faults.*

fern A nonseed plant that has roots, stems, and leaves and that is found mostly in moist, shady areas. (A79) On *ferns* that grow in tropical places, the fronds grow at the top of a tall trunk.

fertilization (furt ′l ə zā′shən) The process by which a male sex cell joins with a female sex cell. In flowering plants, fertilization takes place in the pistil. (A60) *Fertilization* occurs after a pollen tube reaches the ovary.

filter A device that lets certain colors of light pass through while absorbing others. (F18) The stage manager placed a red *filter* over the spotlight.

flower The reproductive structure of a flowering plant. (A16) Petals protect the reproductive parts of a *flower.*

flowering plant Living organisms that reproduce by seeds formed in flowers and that have roots, stems, and leaves. (A81) *Flowering plants* are the most common group of plants on Earth today.

focal point The point at which light rays passing through a lens come together. (F32) Rays of light meet at the *focal point.*

fold A bend in a layer of rock. (E83) Forces within Earth can cause a *fold* to form in rock layers.

food chain The path of energy transfer from one living organism to another in an ecosystem. (A36, D29) Energy moves from producers to consumers in a *food chain.*

food web The overlapping food chains that link producers, consumers, and decomposers in an ecosystem. (A37, D30) Some consumers in a *food web* eat both plants and animals.

force A pull or a push. (C28) When you open a door, you apply a *force.*

fossil (fäs′əl) The remains or traces of a living thing from the past, preserved in rock. (E46, E77) *Fossils* can include imprints of animal skeletons pressed into rock.

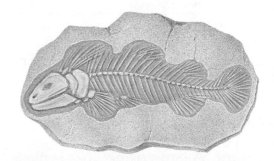

fracture (frak′chər) A break or crack in a bone. (G20) The skier suffered a leg *fracture* when he hit an icy patch.

free fall The motion of a freely falling object, such as a spacecraft in orbit around Earth. (B79) Astronauts experiencing *free fall* in space feel weightless.

frequency (frē′kwən sē) The number of waves (such as light or sound) produced in a unit of time, such as a second. (F18, F57) The *frequency* of light waves varies with the color of the light.

friction (frik′shən) Force produced by the rubbing of one thing against another; a force that acts to oppose motion. (C31) *Friction* prevents sneakers from slipping on a gym floor.

fruit The enlarged ovary of a flower that protects the developing seeds. (A61) Some *fruits*, such as peaches or mangoes, contain only one seed.

fulcrum (ful′krəm) The fixed point around which a lever pivots. (C50) If you use a lever to lift an object, the *fulcrum* is located between you and the object you are lifting.

galaxy (gal′ək sē) A vast group of billions of stars that are held together by gravity. (B70) The Milky Way is a typical spiral *galaxy*.

gas giant A large planet that is made up mostly of gaseous and liquid substances, with little or no solid surface. (B47) Jupiter is a *gas giant*.

geocentric model (jē ō sen′trik mäd″l) A representation of the universe in which stars and planets revolve around Earth. (B37) Ptolemy proposed a *geocentric model* of the universe.

glucose (gloo′kōs) A sugar produced by plants that is the main source of energy for cells. (A33) *Glucose* is produced during photosynthesis.

grassland A biome containing many grasses but few trees and having low to moderate rainfall. (D50) Taller grasses occur in *grasslands* that have more abundant rainfall.

hardness A measure of how easily a mineral can be scratched. (E13) The *hardness* of diamond is greater than that of any other mineral.

hearing aid A small battery-powered electronic device that makes sounds louder. (F86) Most people who wear a *hearing aid* have improved hearing.

heliocentric model (hē lē ō sen′trik mäd″l) A representation of the relationship between the Sun and planets in which the planets revolve around the Sun. (B37) Copernicus hypothesized a *heliocentric model* of the solar system.

herbivore (hʉr′bə vôr) A consumer that eats only plants or other producers. (D19, D30) Panda bears are *herbivores* that have a very limited diet because they only eat bamboo.

hertz (herts) A unit used to measure wave frequency. (F18, F68) If 100 waves are produced per second, the frequency of the wave is 100 *hertz*.

igneous rock (ig′nē əs räk) A type of rock that forms from melted rock that cools and hardens. (E40) *Igneous rock* forms from both magma and lava.

illegal drug A substance whose use is prohibited by law. (G50) One *illegal drug* in the United States is heroin.

inclined plane A simple machine with a sloping surface. It allows objects to be raised or lowered from one level to another without lifting them. (C43) A ramp is a kind of *inclined plane*.

index fossil (in′deks fäs′əl) A fossil used to determine the relative age of rock. (E78) The remains of a living thing that lived only at a certain time in the past makes a good *index fossil*.

information superhighway The futuristic concept of communications as an *electronic highway* system in which telephones, computers, and televisions are linked. (F93) The *information superhighway* will let students do library research from their homes.

intensity (in ten′sə tē) A measure of the amount of energy of sound. (F78) A sound that has high *intensity* is loud enough to be heard from a distance.

Internet (in′tər net) A system of interconnected computer networks. (F94) Telephone lines link computer users with the *Internet*.

joint The place where two bones meet. (G8) Your elbow *joint* enables you to bend your arm.

joule (jo͞ol) The basic unit of energy and of work. (C19) Scientists measure amounts of energy in *joules*.

kinetic energy The energy that something has because of its motion. (C20) As a boulder rolls down a steep hill, it gains *kinetic energy*.

---

lake A freshwater ecosystem characterized by still, or standing water. (D53) *Lakes* support fish, birds, algae, and other forms of life.

lava (lä′və) Melted rock material that reaches Earth's surface before it cools and hardens. (E41) A volcano carries *lava* to Earth's surface.

leaf A plant part in which photosynthesis takes place. (A14) In a plant such as cabbage, it is the *leaf* that people eat.

lens A piece of glass or other transparent material with at least one curved surface that brings together or spreads apart light rays passing through it. (F32) The *lens* in a camera focuses an image on the film.

lever (lev'ər) A simple machine made up of a bar that pivots around a fixed point (a fulcrum). (C50) A *lever* can help lift a heavy object with less effort.

ligament (lig'ə mənt) A band of strong tissue that connects bones and holds them in place. (G8) A *ligament* holds bones together at a joint.

light-year A unit of measurement representing the distance that light travels in one year. (B61) Scientists use the unit called a *light-year* when measuring the distances to stars.

luster (lus'tər) The way that the surface of a mineral looks when it reflects light. (E13) Silver and gold have a shiny, metallic *luster*.

machine A device that makes work easier by reducing the amount of force needed to do a job. (C43) A *machine* can make it easier to move, lift, carry, or cut something.

magma (mag'mə) Melted rock material that forms deep within Earth. (E40) Some igneous rocks, such as granite, form from *magma*.

mantle A thick layer of rock between the crust and the core of Earth. (E69) The top of the *mantle* is solid rock but below that is a section of rock that can flow.

mechanical advantage (mə kan'i-kəl ad vant'ij) The number of times that a machine multiplies the effort force applied to it. (C44) To find the *mechanical advantage* of an inclined plane, divide the length of its sloping surface by its height.

medulla (mi dul'ə) The part of the brain that controls the involuntary functions of the body, such as heart rate and breathing. (G32) The *medulla* is located in the brain stem and controls many things you do without thinking.

metamorphic rock (met ə môr'fik räk) A type of rock that forms from existing rocks because of changes caused by heat, pressure, or chemicals. (E47) Slate is a *metamorphic rock* that forms from the sedimentary rock shale.

meteor (mēt'ē ər) A piece of rock or metal from space that enters Earth's atmosphere. (B25) A *meteor* appears as a streak of light, which is why it is also called a shooting star.

meteorite (mēt'ē ər īt) The remaining material of a meteor that has landed on the ground. (B26) In 1902, scientists were able to examine the largest *meteorite* ever known to land in the United States.

Milky Way Galaxy A gigantic cluster of billions of stars that is home to our solar system. (B70) The Sun is located in one of the arms of the *Milky Way Galaxy.*

mineral A solid element or compound found in nature and having a definite chemical composition and crystal structure. (E12) Quartz is a *mineral.*

model Something used or made to represent an object or an idea. (E68) The plastic *model* airplane was a miniature copy of the actual airplane.

monocot (män'ō kät) A flowering plant that produces seeds with a single seed leaf, or food-storing leaf. (A81) About one third of all flowering plants are *monocots.*

moon A natural object that revolves around a planet. (B44) The planet Mars has two known *moons.*

moss A small nonseed plant that lacks roots, stems, and leaves and grows mostly in moist areas in woods or near stream banks. (A78) The leaflike part of *moss* only grows a few centimeters above ground.

motor neuron (mōt'ər noo'rän) A nerve cell that carries impulses from the brain and spinal cord to muscles and glands in the body. (G28) When people exercise, *motor neurons* carry impulses from the spinal cord to different muscles in the body.

mutualism (myoo'choo əl iz əm) A close relationship between two or more organisms in which all organisms benefit. (D22) Bees carrying pollen from flower to flower as they obtain nectar is an example of *mutualism.*

narcotic (när kät'ik) A habit-forming drug that depresses the function of the nervous system. (G55) Morphine is a *narcotic* drug that is often given to cancer patients.

nebula (neb'yə lə) A huge cloud of gas and dust found in space. (B64) A *nebula* can form when a supernova explodes.

nerve impulse (nʉrv im'puls) A message carried through the body by neurons. (G28) *Nerve impulses* pass from one neuron to another as they move through the body.

neuron (noo'rän) A nerve cell. (G28) The brain is connected to all parts of the body by *neurons.*

neutron star (nōō′trän stär) The remains of a massive star that has exploded in a supernova. (B67) A typical *neutron star* is less than 20 km in diameter.

newton A unit used to measure force. (C29) About 300 *newtons* of force was applied in moving the rock.

nicotine (nik′ə tēn) A drug found in the tobacco plant. (G50) People become addicted to cigarettes because of the *nicotine* in the tobacco.

nitrogen cycle The cycle through which nitrogen gas is changed into compounds that can be used by living things and then is returned to the atmosphere. (D42) The *nitrogen cycle* is of great importance to all life forms because nitrogen is needed to make protein.

noise pollution The occurrence of loud or unpleasant sound in the environment. (F80) The sounds of city traffic are a form of *noise pollution.*

nonseed plant A plant that reproduces without forming seeds. (A78) Mosses are *nonseed plants.*

nucleus (nōō′klē əs) The cell structure that controls all of a cell's activities. (A24) The *nucleus* was clearly visible after it was stained.

octave (äk′tiv) The series of eight notes that makes up a musical scale. (F69) The music student practiced playing *octaves* on the piano.

omnivore (äm′ni vôr) A consumer that eats both plants and animals. (D19, D30) Because they eat both meats and vegetables, many humans are *omnivores.*

opaque (ō pāk′) Not letting light through. (F47) The *opaque* curtains kept out the sunlight.

open ocean A large saltwater ecosystem containing both floating and free-swimming organisms. (D55) The *open ocean* covers much of Earth's surface.

optic nerve A bundle of neurons that carries impulses from the eye to the brain. (G39) If there is damage to the *optic nerve,* messages from the eye cannot be received by the brain.

ore (ôr) A mineral or rock that contains enough of a metal to making mining the metal profitable. (E27) Hemalite is an *ore* mined for its iron content.

overtone A fainter, higher tone that harmonizes with the main tone produced by a musical instrument or the human voice. (F58) The blending of *overtones* gives the flute its unique sound.

oxygen–carbon dioxide cycle A natural cycle in which plants and other producers use carbon dioxide and produce oxygen, and living things use oxygen and produce carbon dioxide. (B86, D34) The *oxygen–carbon dioxide cycle* must be duplicated in space if humans wish to make long voyages to other planets.

parasitism (par′ə sīt iz əm) A relationship between two organisms in which one organism lives on or in the other, feeds upon it, and usually harms it. (D21) The way in which fleas live off dogs is an example of *parasitism*.

phloem cell (flō′əm sel) A plant cell that, when linked with other similar cells, forms a system of tubes for carrying nutrients from the leaves down through the stem and root. (A11) The *phloem cells* form a major transport system in plants.

phonograph (fō′nə graf) A device that reproduces sounds recorded on a disk. (F90) We played old records on the *phonograph*.

photosynthesis (fōt ō sin′thə sis) The process by which producers, such as plants, make their own food by using energy from the Sun. (A33) *Photosynthesis* takes place primarily in the leaves of plants.

pistil (pis′til) The female reproductive structure of a flower. (A16) A *pistil* consists of three main parts—the stigma, the style, and the ovary.

pitch The highness or lowness of a sound. (F68) A tuba produces sounds with a low *pitch*.

plane mirror A mirror that has a flat surface. (F23) The mirror over the bathroom sink is a *plane mirror*.

planet A large body in space that orbits a star and does not produce light on its own. (B17) Earth is one of nine known *planets* that revolve around the Sun.

plant kingdom A major group of living things that are multicellular and that carry out photosynthesis. (A78) Living organisms in the *plant kingdom* make their own food.

pollination (päl ə nā′shən) The transfer of pollen from the male part of one flower to the female part of another flower. (A60) Some *pollination* is done by insects.

population (päp yoo lā′shən) A group of the same kind of organisms that live in an area. (D10) There is a huge *population* of frogs in that marsh.

potential energy The energy that an object has because of its position or structure; stored energy. (C18) A coiled spring has *potential energy*.

precipitation (prē sip ə tā'shən) The process by which water from clouds falls back to the Earth. (D36) *Precipitation* falls to the Earth in the form of rain or snow.

producer (prō dōōs'ər) An organism that makes its own food through photosynthesis. (A36, D18) Plants and algae are examples of *producers*.

protein (prō'tēn) Organic compounds that form the structure and control the processes that take place in living things. (D41) *Proteins* provide the body with materials that help cells grow and repair themselves.

protostar (prōt'ō stär) A concentration of matter found in space that is the beginning of a star. (B64) When the temperature inside a *protostar* becomes high enough, nuclear reactions begin and it turns into a star.

pulley (pōōl'ē) A simple machine made up of a wheel around which a rope or chain is passed. (C53) A *pulley* helps lift objects that would be too heavy to lift directly.

quarry (kwôr'ē) A mine, usually near or at Earth's surface, from which rock is removed. (E52) Granite, sandstone, limestone, slate, and marble are some rocks that come from a *quarry*.

radiation (rā dē ā'shən) The transfer of energy by waves. (C11) Energy given off by the Sun travels as *radiation* through space.

radio telescope A gigantic antenna designed to receive radio signals from space. (B92) *Radio telescopes* are important tools for studying distant stars and galaxies.

rarefaction (rer ə fak'shən) A region in a sound wave where there are fewer particles than normal. (F57) The *rarefactions* that a vibrating violin string produces are areas of lower than normal air pressure.

receptor (ri sep'tər) A sensory neuron that receives stimuli from the environment. (G37) Sensory *receptors* in the skin make it possible for people to feel heat, cold, pressure, touch, and pain.

red giant A very large old reddish star that has greatly expanded and cooled as its fuel has begun to run out. (B65) As the Sun reaches old age, it will turn into a *red giant*.

reflecting telescope An instrument for viewing distant objects that uses a curved mirror at the back of its tube to gather light and produce an image. (B22, F39) This observatory uses a *reflecting telescope* to observe faraway galaxies.

reflection (ri flek′shən) The bouncing of light or sound off a surface. (F22) The *reflection* of sunlight off the snow made us squint.

reflex (rē′fleks) A simple behavior pattern involving an automatic response to a stimulus. (G42) The girl's automatic *reflex* quickly got her foot out of the hot water.

refracting telescope An instrument for viewing distant objects that uses two lenses to gather light and produce an image. (B21) The *refracting telescope* gave us a closer look at the Moon.

refraction (ri frak′shən) The bending of light as it passes from one material into another. (F24) Light traveling from air into water will undergo *refraction*.

relative age The age of an object as compared to other objects. (E78) The order of layers of rock shows the *relative ages* of the layers.

resistance force A force that resists, or opposes, motion. (C30) Friction is a *resistance force*.

retina (ret′′n ə) The light-sensitive area at the back of the eye on which an image is formed. (F34) The *retina* contains two kinds of cells.

revolution (rev ə lōō′shən) The movement of an object around another object or point. (B14) It takes about 365 days for Earth to make one *revolution* around the Sun.

river A freshwater ecosystem characterized by running water. (D52) Salmon are able to swim against the current in a *river*.

rock The solid material composed of minerals that forms Earth's crust. Also, the material, sometimes molten, that forms Earth's inner layers. (E40) *Rocks* are weathered by wind and rain.

rock cycle The continuous series of changes that rocks undergo. (E60) In the *rock cycle*, changes are brought about by factors such as weathering, melting, cooling, or pressure.

root The underground part of a plant that anchors the plant and absorbs water and nutrients. (A10) Carrots and turnips have only one large single *root*.

rotation (rō tā′shən) The spinning motion of an object on its axis. (B14) It takes about 24 hours for Earth to make one complete *rotation*.

S

sapling (sap′liŋ) A young tree. (A67) The year after a tree seed germinates, the young plant is called a *sapling*.

satellite (sat′′l īt) A natural or human-built object that revolves around another object in space. (B44) The Moon is a natural *satellite* of Earth.

sediment (sed′ə mənt) Bits of weathered rocks and minerals and pieces of dead plants or animals. (E43) Over time, *sediments* can form sedimentary rocks, such as sandstone and limestone.

sedimentary rock (sed ə men′tər ē räk) A type of rock that forms when sediments harden. (E43) Most *sedimentary rocks* form in layers.

seed coat A tough, protective covering on a seed, enclosing the embryo and its food supply. (A 61) When the leaves on a young plant start to grow and open up, the *seed coat* falls off.

seed dispersal The scattering of seeds away from the parent plant. (A88) The wind is one way in which *seed dispersal* is carried out.

seed leaf A first leaf found inside a seed, providing food for the tiny developing plant. (A66) A monocot seed contains one *seed leaf*.

seedling (sēd′liŋ) A young growing plant after it first sprouts and develops new leaves. (A66) In spring the forest floor is covered with green *seedlings*.

seed plant A plant that reproduces by forming seeds. (A78) Corn and wheat are *seed plants*.

semicircular canal Any of three curved tubelike structures of the inner ear that help the body to maintain balance. (F85) The *semicircular canals* respond to movements of the head.

sensory neuron (sen′sər ē nōō′rän) A nerve cell that carries impulses from the senses to the brain and spinal cord. (G28) *Sensory neurons* carry impulses from your eyes to your brain.

sexual reproduction The production of offspring that occurs when a male sex cell joins a female sex cell. (A59) The *sexual reproduction* of flowers is greatly aided by insects.

shoreline The ecosystem where land and ocean meet. (D54) The *shoreline* varies in width around the world.

simple microscope A microscope that uses a single lens to magnify objects. (F41) A magnifying glass is a *simple microscope*.

skeletal muscle Voluntary muscle tissue; also, one of the muscles that moves bones. (G17) Tendons attach *skeletal muscles* to bones.

skeletal system The system of bones and tissues that supports and protects the body. (G8) The human *skeletal system* contains 206 bones.

smelting (smelt′iŋ) The process of melting ore to remove the metal from it. (E28) Workers obtain iron by *smelting* iron ore in a blast furnace.

smooth muscle Involuntary muscle tissue that lines the inside of blood vessels, intestines, and other organs. (G17) *Smooth muscles* move food through the digestive system.

solar system The Sun and the planets and other objects that orbit the Sun. Also, any star and the objects that revolve around it. (B34) Our *solar system* consists of the Sun, nine known planets, and many smaller objects.

sound A form of energy that travels through matter as waves. (F56) The *sound* made the floor vibrate.

sound synthesizer (sound sin′thə sī zər) An electronic device that can produce a wide variety of sounds. (F71) The composer used a *sound synthesizer* to create a new musical composition.

sprain An injury in which the ligament at a joint is torn or twisted. (G19) An ankle *sprain* can take weeks to heal.

stamen (stā′mən) The male reproductive structure of a flower. (A16) Pollen is produced in the *stamens*.

star A huge object in space, made up of hot gases, that shines by its own light. (B17) Many *stars* are believed to have systems of planets.

starch (stärch) A substance found in plants that is a storage form of glucose. (A35) Potatoes contain a lot of *starch*.

stem The part of a plant that supports the leaves and flowers and carries water to these parts of the plant. (A12) The trunk of a tree is a *stem*.

steroid (stir′oid) A drug that helps to build up muscle tissue and strength. (G55) Some athletes have used *steroids*.

stimulant (stim′yo͞o lənt) A drug that increases the activity of the nervous system. (G55) Many people drink coffee because it acts as a *stimulant*.

stimulus (stim′yo͞o ləs) An event or environmental condition that triggers a nerve impulse, thus causing an organism to respond. (G28) The *stimulus* of a loud sound can make a person jump.

stoma (stō′mə; *pl.* stō ma′tə) One of many small openings, or pores, usually on the underside of a leaf, through which gases enter and leave a plant. (A46) The *stomata* on a water lily are on the top of the leaf.

strain An injury in which a muscle or tendon is torn slightly or stretched too far. (G20) Lifting the heavy couch gave me a back *strain*.

streak (strēk) The colored powder made by rubbing a mineral against a ceramic surface. (E15) Although pyrite is yellow, it produces a black *streak*.

substance abuse (sub′stəns ə-byo͞os′) The improper use, or abuse, of alcohol or drugs. (G50) *Substance abuse* can damage a person's health.

supernova (so͞o′pər nō və) An exploding star. (B66) When a red giant star uses up all its fuel, it collapses and explodes in a *supernova*.

syncline (sin′klīn) A downward fold of rock layers. (E84) Forces in Earth pushing on rock formed a *syncline*.

T

taiga (tī'gə) A biome that contains many coniferous trees and in which rainfall is moderate. (D51) The *taiga* is south of the tundra.

taste bud A receptor on the surface of the tongue that responds to different substances and makes it possible to taste. (G38) There are only four basic types of *taste buds*.

tendon (ten'dən) A strong cord of tissue that joins a muscle to a bone. (G17) *Tendons* pull on bones like strings pull on the limbs of a puppet.

terrestrial planet (tə res'trē əl plan'it) An object in space that resembles Earth in size, in density, and in its mainly rocky composition. (B44) Mars is a *terrestrial planet*.

timbre (tam'bər) The quality of sound that sets one voice or musical instrument apart from another. (F58) The same note played on a violin and on a trumpet differ in *timbre*.

translucent (trans lo͞o'sənt) Letting light through but scattering it; objects cannot be clearly seen through translucent material. (F48) The *translucent* glass dimmed the room.

transparent (trans per'ənt) Letting light through; objects can be clearly seen through transparent material. (F47) Window glass is usually *transparent* so that people can see through it.

transpiration (tran spə rā'shən) A process in which a plant releases moisture through its stomata. (A46) *Transpiration* adds water to the air.

tropical rain forest A biome distinguished by lush vegetation, abundant rainfall, and plentiful sunlight. (D50) The *tropical rain forest* supports the greatest variety of life of any biome.

tropism (trō'piz əm) A growth response of a plant to conditions in the environment, such as light or water. (A50) Growing toward a light source is an example of a plant *tropism*.

trough (trôf) The long narrow hollow between two waves. (F57) A *trough* occurs between two wave crests.

tundra (tun'drə) A biome characterized by cold temperatures and low precipitation. (D51) The *tundra* blooms in summer.

U

universe (yo͞on'ə vʉrs) The sum of everything that exists. (B70) Our solar system is part of the *universe*.

V

vacuole (vak'yo͞o ōl) A cell part that stores water and nutrients. (A24) Some plant cells have large *vacuoles*.

vacuum (vak′y$\overline{oo}$ əm) A space that is empty of any matter. (F17) Light waves can travel through a *vacuum.*

vibration A back-and-forth movement of matter. (F56) It is the *vibration* of the guitar strings that produces sound.

visible light A form of electromagnetic energy that can be seen. (F8) The eye responds to *visible light.*

volume The loudness or softness of a sound. (F78) Please turn up the *volume* on the radio.

water cycle A continuous process in which water moves between the atmosphere and Earth's surface, including its use by living things. (B87, D36) The *water cycle* is powered by energy from the Sun.

wave A disturbance that carries energy and that travels away from its starting point. (F17) The experiment measured how quickly light *waves* travel.

wavelength The distance between one crest of a wave and the next crest. (F17, F57) Red light has a longer *wavelength* than does blue light.

weathering The breaking up of rocks into sediments by such forces as wind, rain, and sunlight. (E62) Through *weathering,* igneous rock can be broken down into sediments.

wetland Any one of three ecosystems—marsh, swamp, or bog—where land and fresh water meet. (D53) *Wetlands* help purify water.

wheel and axle A simple machine made of two wheels of different sizes that pivot around the same point. (C58) A doorknob, along with its shaft, is an example of a *wheel and axle.*

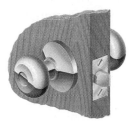 

white dwarf A very small, dying star that gives off very little light. (B65) When the Sun's fuel runs out, it will collapse into a *white dwarf.*

work The movement of a force through a distance. (C28) *Work* is done in lifting an object.

xylem cell (zī′ləm sel) A plant cell that, when joined with other similar cells, forms a transport system throughout a plant. (A11) The wood of a tree is formed mainly of *xylem cells.*

INDEX

* Activity

* Activity

CREDITS

Cover: *Design, Art Direction, and Production:* Design Five, NYC; *Photography:* Jade Albert; *Photography Production:* Picture It Corporation; *Illustration:* Deborah Haley Melmon. **TOC:** Dom Doyle, Patrick Gnan, Robert Pasternack, Michael Sloan, Elsa Warnick.

ILLUSTRATORS

UNIT 5A Chapter A1: Steve Buchanan: 12, 13, 15; Susan Johnston Carlson: 25; Fran Milner 24, 27; Patrick O'Brien: 18, 19, 20, 21; Walter Stuart: 10, 11. **Chapter A2:** David Barber: 38; Barbara Cousins: 34; Brad Gaber: 47; Patrick Gnan: 50, 51, 52; Carlyn Iverson: 36, 39; Merri Nelson: 46; Mary Ellen Niatas: 44, 45; Debra Page-Trim: 37. **Chapter A3:** Glory Bechtold: 59, 60, 61; Catherine Deeter: 66, 67; Eldon Doty: 68, 69; Wendy Smith-Griswold: 73. **Chapter A4:** Jennifer Hewitson: 82, 83; Karen Minot: 90, 91; Merri Nelson: 88, 89; Wendy Smith-Griswold: 78, 82, 83, 95; Elsa Warnick: 92, 93.

UNIT 5B Chapter B1: Delores Bego: 9; Michael Carroll: 14; Dale Glasgow & Assoc.: 10, 11; Jeff Hitch: 13; Fred Holz: 22; Tony Novak: 15; Tom Powers: 11, 27; Robert Schuster: 17; Jim Starr: 24, 25; Lane Yerkes: 21. **Chapter B2:** Michael Carroll: 38, 39, 50; Dennis Davidson: 34, 35, 42, 43; Dale Glasgow & Assoc.: 30, 36, 37, 40, 50; Joe LeMonnier: 72; Susan Melrath: 36, 37; Verlin Miller: 36; John O'Connor: 41; Robert Schuster: 44, 45, 47, 48, 49, 50. **Chapter B3:** Michael Carroll: 70; Joe LeMonnier: 72; Lu Matthews: 60, 61; Tom Powers: 57, 67, 71, 73; Joe Spencer: 64, 65. **Chapter B4:** Terry Boles: 79; Richard Courtney: 87; Dale Glasgow & Assoc.: 94; Nina Laden: 84; Andy Myer: 93; Scott Ross: 83; Stephen Wagner: 80, 86, 95.

UNIT 5C Chapter C1: Delores Bego: 35; Kieran Bergin: 18, 19; Ka Botzis: 22; Carolyn Bracken: 12; Sarah Jane English: 22, 23; Ron Fleming: 12; David Uhl: 20, 21; Arden Von Haeger: 32, 33; Richard Waldrep: 28, 29. **Chapter C2:** Andrea Baruffi: 43; Gregg Fitzhugh: 48, 49, 53, 54, 55, 63; Dale Glasgow & Assoc.: 50, 51; Patrick Gnan: 58, 59; Susan Hunt Yule: 44, 45; A. J. Miller: 60; Miles Parnell: 43, 44, 45; Michael Sloan: 61, 62; Leslie Wolf: 53, 54.

UNIT 5D Chapter D1: Lori Anzalone: 20; Patrick Gnan: 8, 9; Robert Hynes Studio: 10, 11; Jim Salvati: 12, 13; Wendy Smith-Griswold: 17. **Chapter D2:** David Barber: 28; Andy Lendway: 30, 31, 43; Jim Starr: 38; Don Stewart: 34, 35, 36, 37, 41, 42. **Chapter D3:** Joe LeMonnier: 56; Paul Mirocha: 52, 53, 54, 55; Carlos Ochagauia: 59; Rodica Prato: 48, 49, 50, 51.

UNIT 5E Chapter E1: Jeanette Adams: 28; Lingta Kung: 12, 13, 14, 15, 16; Bill Morse: 30, 31; Wendy Smith-Griswold: 20, 21. **Chapter E2:** Terry Boles: 61, 63; Brad Gaber: 40, 58, 59; Robert Pasternack: 47; Scot Ritchie: 54; Robert Schuster: 49; Michael Sloan: 60. **Chapter E3:** Absolute Science: 71, 77; Eldon Doty: 76; Dale Glasgow & Assoc.: 68, 69, 95; J.A.K. Graphics: 78; Joe LeMonnier: 85, 93; Susan Melrath: 78, 79; Verlin Miller: 86; Robert Pasternack: 85, 91; Tom Powers: 67; Scot Ritchie: 70; Jim Starr: 87.

UNIT 5F Chapter F1: Jeanette Adams: 16; Bob Brugger: 25, 27; Michael Carroll: 8, 9; Jim Deigan: 22; Eldon Doty: 12; Susan Hunt Yule: 26; Robert Pasternack: 17, 18, 19; Scot Ritchie: 8. **Chapter F2:** Rose Berlin: 51; Bob Bredemeier: 39; Marie Dauenheimer: 33, 35; Jim Fanning: 45; J.A.K. Graphics: 32, 34; George Kelvin: 36, 37; Andy Miller: 43; Len Morgan: 47. **Chapter F3:** Mark Bender: 69; Terry Boles: 62, 63; Roger Chandler: 68, 69; Dale Glasgow & Assoc.: 56, 57, 59; Tom Lochray: 66, 67; Larry Moore: 71, 72; Terry Ravanelli: 72. **Chapter F4:** Tim Blough: 94; Marty Bucella: 78; Dale Glasgow & Assoc.: 93, 94; Dale Gustafson: 91, 92; Ellen Going Jacobs: 85; Ray Vella: 78, 79, 95.

UNIT 5G Chapter G1: May Cheney: 8, 9, 10, 11; Kathleen Dunne: 8, 19, 20, 21, 22; Jackie Heda: 12, 19, 20; Bob Swanson: 13; Kate Sweeney: 17, 18, 23. **Chapter G2:** Scott Barrows: 30, 31; Eldon Doty: 40, 41; Dom Doyle: 28; Marcia Hartsock: 37, 38, 39, 42, 45; Jackie Heda: 31; Jane Hurd: 31, 32; Robert Margulies: 33; Steve McInturff: 44; Briar Lee Mitchell: 29. **Chapter G3:** Medical Art Co.: 59, 63; Bob Novak: 50, 51, 53; Ray Vella: 52, 61.

Glossary: Lori Anzalone, Patrick Gnan, Carlyn Iverson, Fran Milner, Robert Pasternack.

Handbook: Kathleen Dunne, Laurie Hamilton, Catherine Leary, Andy Meyer.

PHOTOGRAPHS
All photographs by Silver Burdett Ginn (SBG) unless otherwise noted.

Unit A Opener 1: *border* G. Shih-R. Kessel/Visuals Unlimited. **Chapter 1 4–5:** *bkgd.* Will Houghton/Fairchild Tropical Garden, Miami; *insets* Courtesy, Fairchild Tropical Gardens. 6–9: Ken Karp for SBG. 10: Alfred Pasieka/Peter Arnold. 12: © John Buitenkant/Photo Researchers, Inc. 13: © Cecil Fox/Science Source/Photo Researchers, Inc. 14: *t.* © Jerome Wexler/Photo Researchers, Inc.; *b.* Milton Rand/Tom Stack & Associates. 15: *l.* Milton Rand/Tom Stack & Associates; *r.* © Scott Camamzine/Photo Researchers, Inc. 16: *l.* E. R. Degginger/Color-Pic, Inc.; *r.* © Arthur Beck/Photo Researchers, Inc. 17: *t.* © Anthony Mercieca/Photo Researchers, Inc.; *b.l.* Brokaw Photography/Visuals Unlimited; *b.m.* Rod Planck/Tom Stack & Associates; *b.r.* John Gerlach/Visuals Unlimited. 19: *t.* © Blair Seitz/Photo Researchers, Inc.; *b.* Gary Milburn/Tom Stack & Associates; *inset*